GLASS BARWARE

Deco & Beyond

WALTER T. LEMISKI

Schiffer Publishing Ltd®

4880 Lower Valley Road, Atglen, PA 19310 USA

Dedication

Here's to my beloved parents, Bernice and Wally, who instilled me with a thirst for knowledge.

May your glass be ever full.
May the roof over your head be always strong.
And may you be in heaven
Half an hour before the devil knows you're dead.

—Old Irish Toast

Published by Schiffer Publishing Ltd.
4880 Lower Valley Road
Atglen, PA 19310
Phone: (610) 593-1777; Fax: (610) 593-2002
E-mail: Info@schifferbooks.com

For the largest selection of fine reference books on this and related subjects, please visit our web site at **www.schifferbooks.com**
We are always looking for people to write books on new and related subjects. If you have an idea for a book please contact us at the above address.

This book may be purchased from the publisher.
Include $3.95 for shipping.
Please try your bookstore first.
You may write for a free catalog.

In Europe, Schiffer books are distributed by
Bushwood Books
6 Marksbury Ave.
Kew Gardens
Surrey TW9 4JF England
Phone: 44 (0) 20 8392-8585; Fax: 44 (0) 20 8392-9876
E-mail: info@bushwoodbooks.co.uk
Free postage in the U.K., Europe; air mail at cost.

Library of Congress Control Number: 2005936347

Cover and book designed by Bruce Waters
Type set in Exotic Bold BT/Aldine 721 BT

ISBN: 0-7643-2415-2
Printed in China
1 2 3 4

Contents

Dear Readers

Besides the gent's fedoras, the elegant cocktail dresses, and the amazing hats of the ladies, I can recall—when I was a wee lad—the wonderland of 1960s house parties. I can also remember a few select barware items that I thought were oh so neat. One such memory is of a little frosted crystal whiskey tumbler with red lettering and an HA logo on the bottom. This "Say When Steps" tumbler was marked with measurements from zero to four ounces, with a rabbit at zero, a stick figure gal at one toasting the stick figure gentleman with his jaunty top hat on the second step, a pig on the third level, and finally a hic-hawing donkey marking the 4 oz. shot—what great fun! Stuck in my memory too are the decorated cocktail shakers with recipes, pink pigs, or pheasants; and the retro decorated pilsener glasses with geometric forms evoking the ultra modernity of that era. Those were my first memories of barware.

Like so many before me, I suspect that I have attempted to recapture those fond memories through collecting some of that funky barware. As my collecting progressed, I discovered the sophisticated cocktail ware of the 1940s and the masterpieces of 1920s and '30s glassware—from aesthetic masterpieces to the whimsical. I continue to be dazzled by the phenomenal range of ingenuity, innovation, and artistry that glass masters of the twentieth century were able to conjure up through barware in glass.

The author began his beverage researches at a tender age.

I have spent a goodly chunk of time poring over old catalogues and many collector books attempting to fill in as many details about the barware pictured here as possible. Many authors, collectors, and dealers also were kind enough to share their knowledge and precious items from their collections. Ultimately, I accept responsibility for the final identifications. I have attempted not to make too many leaps of faith in assigning company names to items. I thought that dealing with a mere twenty glass companies in my last book was tricky enough—in this present volume the number is around fifty! My hope is that misattributions are minimal. However, should you be able to identify any mystery items or suggest corrections I'd be most interested to hear from you. As well, if I've missed any of your favorite items in this volume or if you have a collection of barware or some original catalogues or advertising that you'd like to share in future publications, please contact me.

Cheers,
Walt Lemiski
walt@waltztime.com
www.waltztime.com

Acknowledgments

To Lynn and Gerry Mantione, for their wonderful friendship through glass collecting. Special thanks to Lynn (the President of the Depression Glass Club of Rochester) for arranging photo sessions of terrific barware items from the collections of many wonderful club members. The annual Rochester DG Show & Sale each September is one not to be missed!

To Barbara and Jim Mauzy, for their unending support in my striving to learn the art of book building. As prolific authors, their vast knowledge and experience has been of immeasurable help.

To my wonderfully supportive family: my son Nicholas, who takes a keen interest in my collecting world; to wee McDuff, our White West Highland Terrier, who kept me company while writing for so many late nights; and to my beloved wife and helpmate Kimberley, who has been a godsend at numerous photo shoots and whose support is ever steadfast.

To the super collectors, glass dealers, and fine friends who shared their knowledge and opened up their superb collections for legions of fellow collectors to admire—a thousand thanks: Russ Barker, Dale Basaraba, Brenda Beckett, Jennie Bergman, Jean and Wayne Boyd, Vi and Ken Brennan, Norma Brown, David Cooper, Jeff and Mary Czech, Patrick Doherty, Patricia Drumright, Lynda Edwards, Suzanne Fry, Joan Gerber, Donna Hatch, Lesley Hiscoe, Francois Houle, Michael Jameson, Pat Kurtz, Roger LeBlanc, Steve Lindsay, Kathy McCarney, Doris McMullen, Valerie and Bill McCormack, Dave and Hilda Proctor, and Tracy Wills.

To Randy Goldman, whose superb knowledge of the era and inquiring mind opened many new avenues to research.

To Rob Kerr, whose grammatical prowess and ability to hold a pint helped my text gain clarity and cohesion.

To Susan and Manny Alvarez, and Leslie Donovan of the Edward Harris House in Rochester, New York: many thanks for making our stay and our photo sessions there a delightful experience in turn-of-the-century splendor.

To Donna Baker, my editor, a thousand thanks for her insights and great care taken in preparation of this volume.

To the many fellow glass researchers who without reservation have shared knowledge and assisted in verification of facts to make this book as accurate as possible:

Myrna Garrison, Imperial Glass
Ed Goshe, Tiffin Glass
Roger and Claudia Hardy, Akro Agate
Michael Krumme, Paden City Glass
Dick Marsh, Heisey Glass
Emily Seate, Fostoria Glass
Lynn Welker, Cambridge Glass

I drink to your health when I'm with you,
I drink to your health when I'm alone,
I drink to your health so often,
I'm starting to worry about my own.

—Old Irish Toast

Notes on Using this Book

When known, the terms from original company catalogues have been utilized. It is felt that the charm and delight inherent in early variations of terminology would be sorely missed if one tried to codify all item terms. Variations in naming items occur among the numerous glass companies. Even within a single company's nomenclature over the years one can find nifty marketing variations for the same item type. For example: Ice bucket = ice pack = ice tub. Tall sherbet = high sherbet = saucer champagne.

Since much of the glassware in this volume was handmade it is common to observe variations of half an inch or more on various items. Measurements of items are for height unless otherwise indicated.

Fenton #1620 "Plymouth" (1933-37) crystal: old fashioned tumbler, 7 oz., 3-1/2", $12; tumbler, 3-3/4", 5 oz., $10; ice bucket, 6", $45; jigger, 1 oz. and 2 oz., 3-3/4", $45; pilsener, 10 oz., $20. Fenton offered "Plymouth" in 1933 as a "44 Piece Repeal Set." *Courtesy of Donna Hatch.*

About Pricing Barware

Pricing, as anyone in the field can attest to, is a tricky if not treacherous pastime. Having been involved in buying and selling thousands of vintage glass items over the past dozen years has gained me a little insight. Pricing has also been tracked at Depression Glass Shows (probably the best source for finding quality glassware at fair market value from reputable and knowledgeable dealers), general line shows, malls, shops, at live auctions, in the *Canadian Depression Glass Review*, on eBay, and through consultation with major dealers and collectors from coast to coast. Values suggested are for items in mint condition. Chips, cracks, or other damage will significantly lower a piece's value.

Sometimes, the more I talk with various people about pricing glass, the more perplexed I become! My aim in pricing glassware is to come up with a fair market value—a price that ideally most collectors would say to themselves, "Yes, that is a fair price that I'd pay for that item." This is tricky.

On my shelves are many specialist books with prices at which I gasp. There are other books, on the other hand, that make me wonder if and where I could ever find such bargain-basement prices. As most any auction-goer (or on-line observer) has noted, it simply "takes two to tango." In antiquing terms, if two folks are keen to fill a gap in their collections, then fair market pricing goes out the window. Many specialists at times tend to price things higher than generalist collectors. However, specialists may also know how abundant certain items are and value them substantially lower than most general-line dealers. This isn't easy now, is it? Add into the mix regional variations. Even with the mitigating effect of Internet sales, we do still see distinct regional price variations. In a very broad simplification, west coast prices tend to be higher than east coast prices, southern prices tend to be higher than northern prices. All that being said...I am deeply indebted to the many collectors and dealers from coast to coast who have so freely given of their time and knowledge in assisting me with this pricing puzzle.

As mentioned ealier, I hope to be in the right ballpark on pricing. The prices give a reflection of the market at the time of writing. In the words of one of my mentors, "Pricing is a personal matter." What I present is simply my interpretation of the market as I see it for this snapshot of time.

This book is intended only to be a guide for determination of an item's value. One must ultimately decide for oneself just how desirable a certain piece is for one's own collection. Neither the author or publishers assume any responsibility for any transactions that may occur because of this book.

Introduction

Fenton #1611 "Georgian" (1931-42) ruby claret, 4-1/2 oz., $15; green cordial, 1 oz., $15; ruby goblet, 10 oz., $20; ruby cordial, 1 oz., $20; #1620 "Plymouth" (1933-37) Stiegel green sherbet, 4-3/4", $15. *Courtesy of Donna Hatch.*

I cannot begin to imagine what a complete vintage barware pattern reference would look like. It would probably dwarf the monumental *Oxford English Dictionary*! Even if one restricted the main scope of this volume to the 1930s, following the end of Prohibition in 1933—the heyday of barware—one would find much more than could be shown in any one volume. In their *Crystal Stemware Identification Guide*, Bob Page and Dale Frederiksen illustrate shapes and patterns from dozens of glass companies, including several of the major American glass manufacturers. In surveying one of the bigger firms, the Fostoria Glass Company, one spots over 550 different listings. The authors state, "While not trying to be a comprehensive pattern guide on any one manufacturer, it represents a vast majority of the most collectible and requested stemware patterns..." Typically, Fostoria produced at least six or eight sizes for each pattern and several different colors. The numbers are staggering. Needless to say...attempting to identify stemware is liable to drive one to drink!

In 1938, the Tiffin Glass Company produced a 32-page booklet suggesting tips for *How to Give Glamour to Your Table*. In it appear table settings resplendent with Tiffin glassware arranged by Lynne Leslie. The section entitled "Your Beverage Glasses" shows the correct type of stems and glassware for every beverage and notes: "When choosing your glassware in the first place, always demand the best. It's a comfort to know that your taste is unassailable, and besides it's pure economy. The fastidious prefer clear crystal, because colored glass obscures the color of your wines or liqueurs, and the connoisseur regards the color of a wine as an important part of its virtue. While the oldsters sometimes prefer a hollow stem for their champagne and other sparkling wines, the newest trend is toward the champagne flute or saucer. Whatever your choice, you can obtain it in Tiffin's exquisite stemware."

How quickly tastes do change. It was only a dozen years earlier that commentators were hailing the arrival of color in a big way on the glass scene. In the September 1929 issue of the influential homemaker's magazine *Better Homes and Gardens* appeared an article entitled "Serve It in Colored Glassware." The author declared that: "The aristocracy of colored glassware is in its richness and warmness, and the former preponderance of the frigid and sheer-crystal glassware on our table wholly lacked this. Whatever it is, serve it in glass!"

In later years, there appears to have been achieved a balance between appreciation of colored glassware and crystal. The New York based decorative arts scholar, Amelia Leavitt Hill, the Martha Stewart of her era, penned in 1949 her volume *The Complete Book of Table Setting with Service, Etiquette and Flower Arrangement.* Mrs. Hill asks, "What about the color of your glass? That's a question for your own taste. Clear glass is always appropriate; but especially in the informal alcove or breakfast room, colored glass is cheerful and suitable at almost any time. Full dinner services of colored glass are inexpensive and especially popular in summer.

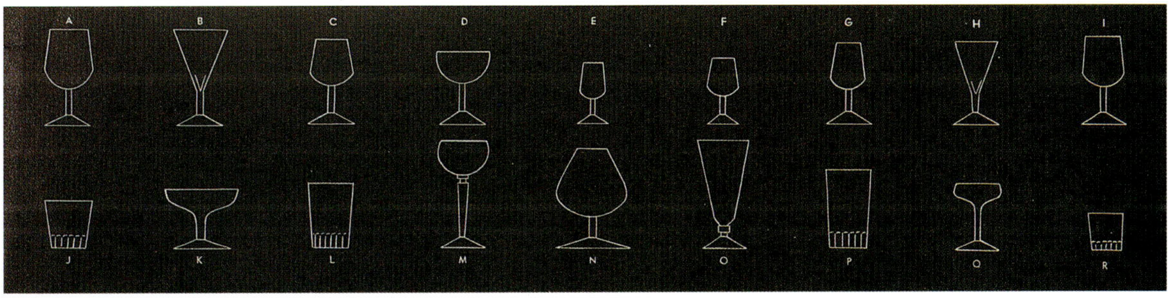

Illustration from Tiffin pamphlet, *How To Give Glamour to Your Table* (1938). A. Water Goblet; B. Champagne Flute; C. Standard Wine; D. Cocktail; E. Liqueur; F. Port Wine; G. Secondary Wine; H. Sherry; I. Great Burgundy; J. Old-Fashioned; K. Saucer Champagne; L. Highball; M. Rhine Wine; N. Brandy Inhaler; O. Footed Beer; P. Brandy and Soda; Q. Crème de Menthe; R. Whiskey. *Author's collection.*

All your glassware need not be alike unless you wish…and though every piece of a variety should resemble all the rest, you need not seek uniformity throughout the entire table setting." These words certainly seen prophetic when considering the eclectic trends of recent years.

Tiffin #17399 "Cherokee Rose" (c.1941) stemware from original catalogue page.

In 1920, a new underground was formed…that of drinkers. By a single stroke of the legislative pen, millions of previously law-abiding American citizens were made into law-breakers. It was the "Great Experiment," that great leap of faith that every man and woman would now become teetotalers.

Many folks across the country were against Prohibition right from its imposition. Drinking was inextricably tied up with the socializing of countless generations of immigrants from Germany, Italy, Poland, and elsewhere. Taverns often were main centers of information and, in some instances, the location where municipal affairs were conducted. Drinking was about much more than getting inebriated—it was about hospitality, generosity, honor, leisure, manliness, and conviviality. On top of this, many thousands of peoples' livelihoods were taken away as the country went "dry." After a spell, many cities and counties across the States largely ignored the new laws; after all, there was no infusion of money or manpower to assist with implementing all the new regulations. More important public safety issues still needed to be dealt with.

In Stephen R. Powell's article "A Little Illegal Holiday Cheer" (1996), in *The Buffalonian*, the author stated that "Buffalo was said by some to be one of the "wettest" cities in America. There was so much illegal booze around that authorities must have felt like they were trying to empty a bathtub filled with liquor one shot-glass at a time." In Buffalo during that time, there resided a certain Francis Xavier Schwab. From the teens he had been a highly successful salesman for a liquor distributor, and had moved on to manage and eventually hold stakes in several breweries. In 1919, with the pending imposition of Prohibition, Schwab was named president and general manager of the Mohawk Products Company (the new name for the merged Buffalo Brewing Company and the Cooperative Brewing Company). The new company was set up to make low alcohol near-beer. By 1920, however, Schwab was accused of making real beer. He was able to delay the inevitable for several years. Meantime, he was convinced to run for the mayoralty of Buffalo. The two main planks of his platform were accessibility, listening to his fellow citizens, and a promise to return light wines and beer to his constituents. Though veteran politicians scoffed that Schwab dare run, he was lo and behold voted in as mayor. One of his first moves was to dismiss the vice and dry squads of the police department. In Schwab's words, "They ought to be out catching crooks, not snooping around." In April of 1922, Mohawk Products Company was ordered to pay $10,000 in back taxes as a settlement against the company. In May of 1922, the new mayor joined police in visiting eleven clubs to check for alcohol—but found no laws being broken. Finally, after much delay, Schwab was charged with involvement with bootlegging. He pleaded

Cover of souvenir photo booklet from "Chez Ami" (c.1945), Buffalo, New York, "Home of the Revolving Bar." *Courtesy of Randy Goldman.*

"no contest" and paid a $500 fine. Today, one would expect that such a scandal would be the end of any politician. Not so for F. X. Schwab—he was subsequently reelected to a second term. Schwab estimated that there were 8,000 "soft drink" establishments in Buffalo alone, which he believed doubled as speakeasies (those disreputable dens of illegal drinking). He served as mayor from 1922-29, letting it be known that he would return to the liquor industry as soon as Prohibition ended.

Coming just a few years after the great stock market crash of 1929, the repeal of the 18th Amendment in 1933, which meant the end of dry America's Prohibition years, was a godsend for glass companies. Many firms had closed up in the late 1920s and early '30s and many others were just hanging on. Although the stock market hit rock bottom mid way through 1932 and things were not quite as bleak, glass historians have pointed to 1933 as the year that saved many glass manufacturers.

Barware had been sold non-stop throughout Prohibition. In 1929, The United States Glass Company went so far as to advertise a patriotic sounding "Uncle Sam" cocktail set consisting of a handled shaker and six footed cocktail glasses. Repeal meant that the floodgates could now open on an astounding range of new barware. With so many firms pinning their survival hopes on this event, designs had to be unique and eye-catching, with the ability to stand out from the crowd. Duncan Miller Glass Company of Washington, Pennsylvania felt they had the right combination with their "Chanticleer" barware—"The glass that cheers Dealers because it Charms Customers." In a 1934 trade advertisement they crowed: "Endless variety is characteristic of all liquor ware displays today—so any new pattern that 'stands out' must be sensational. That's why we're 'crowing' about dealer reports on our Chanticleer liquor line. The rooster embossed design is novel—the perfection of detail and the graceful shapes in Duncan flawless glass make it unmistakably quality ware. Gleaming Chromium tops and spoons of the Shakers and Mixers accent the colors in which Duncan offers Chanticleer—Green, Ruby, Blue, Amber (particularly fine), and Crystal ... A favorite with both men and women—Chanticleer means better sales and mounting profits for you."

During Prohibition, one of the most famous of cocktail books, *The Savoy Cocktail Book*, by Harry Craddock of the Savoy Hotel London, was published in Britain. Although a small number of cocktail recipe books were also available prior to the end of Prohibition, 1933 onwards saw a slew of publications. These included Schenley Product's *Merry Mixer*, first edition 1933, of which—by the 1936 release of the second edition—the company proudly boasted of having distributed over 2 million copies. Starting in 1935, the longest running bar guide is *Old Mr. Boston Official Bartenders Guide*—amazingly still being published and currently closing in on its 70th edition. It is fascinating to flip back through various editions to observe the changes in styles.

Morgantown "Chanticleer" selection. *Courtesy of Jeff & Mary Czech.*

In 1934, Harman Burney Burke published *Burke's Complete Cocktail & Drinking Recipes*. Included was a listing of the world's ten most famous cocktails of 1934:

1. Martini
2. Manhattan Cocktail
3. Bronx Cocktail
4. Old Fashioned Whiskey Cocktail
5. Sidecar Cocktail
6. Clover Club Cocktail
7. Gin Rickey
8. Gin Fizz
9. Bacardi Cocktail
10. Alexander Cocktail

Irvinware cocktail set. *Courtesy of David C. Cooper.*

Hand in glove with the drinks of that era was the cigarette. Imagine what it must have been like to visit one of your favorite haunts back in those days. Your anticipation of a good time, a chance to forget the stark reality of the Depression, was heightened as soon as you heard the dreamy dark tones of your favorite jazz singer as she sang the blues in a most sultry manner, backed up by a red hot trio. Through the blue haze of smoke you'd recognize friends and rubberneck as a starlet or two pranced on by. Everyone is so merry and looks oh so debonair as they sip their cocktails and puff on their Camels.

If I could have included a music CD with this book it would have been one with Frank Sinatra singing that fine Cole Porter standard, "At Long Last Love" (1937). What can be closer to the height of sophistication than ol' Blue Eyes crooning "Is it a cocktail this feeling of joy, or is what I feel the real McCoy?" The lyrics may not mean much to us nowadays, but "McCoy" would have had a real resonance back in that era. Rum-running (sneaking illicit alcohol across the border into the dry States) was in part jump-started on the American east coast by the 1922 Fordney-McCumber tariff. Brought in as a defense against an expected flood of European exports, the tariff imposed new duties on fish products, and Canadian fishermen were prohibited from landing their catches at U.S. ports. Large numbers of fishermen were put out of work and, with no prospects in sight, put their sailing skills to work supplying alcohol to America. One of the fabled stories of the Prohibition era was that of William F. McCoy of Lunenburg, Nova Scotia, Canada. An able sea captain and entrepreneur, McCoy saw the great prospects of rum-running. He also saw the risks and sought to reduce them as the loose border started to tighten up through the 1920s. His ploy was to sail his yacht, the *Arethusia* (outfitted with armor plate and bulletproof glass), down the east coast of the United States, all the time staying out in international waters where he could not be prosecuted. Intrepid American bootleggers from the mainland would come out to his yacht in small speedboats to take supplies in to their thirsty nation. The quality of McCoy's liquor was renowned and reverently guaranteed to be "the real McCoy." The McCoy quality was so highly thought of since there were unscrupulous connivers who would water down the hootch to get a few more dollars. And who were you going to complain to? Certainly not to the authorities. Home brews, so called bathtub gin and gut-rot, could be deadly. More than a few tragic accounts are recorded in newspapers of the day about tipplers dying from bad liquor. Industrial alcohol was even sold to the unsuspecting and was merrily quaffed by those unaware of their pending demise.

To pass a law is one thing, to be able to maintain it is yet another. Trying to control the flood of illicit beverages across the Great Lakes was one such example. The longest unpatrolled border in the world created the greatest opportunity to travel across undetected with truck or car-loads of liquor. Oh yes, the back seats of autos would be removed to accommodate more hootch. It took many years before the borders along the Great Lakes were in any stretch well tended. Eventually, the watchful eyes grew from a mere handful of launches patrolling the lengthy waterways to a flotilla of several hundred artillery-equipped patrol boats. All the while, the intrepid smugglers were perfecting the art of hiding bottles in custom-made clothing, filling eggs with liquor (fine until you dropped some eggs!), pulling cartons across on underwater cables, and crossing waterways when they were frozen in the winter, amongst other novel means.

One major loophole in Canadian laws, which arose when authorities did attempt to assist the American government, was that certain laws were not worded tightly enough. Although midway through the 1920s the Canadian federal government made transporting alcohol to the United States illegal, exports could still go to other countries. Thus, a small boat could dock at a Canadian inland port with proper documentation allowing export of alcohol to a location such as Cuba. The boat would be loaded up and sent underway. After a little sojourn over to the States, the same boat could be back within 48 hours for another load! The end of the absurdity and the end of Prohibition came with Franklin D. Roosevelt's words, "What America needs now is a drink."

Whether you are a teetotaler or an enthusiastic imbiber of the elixir of life, barware in glass is a splendid sight. For a cocktail, a spot of bubbly, a fine wine, or a brew, there is nothing in my mind's eye that is superior to a beverage in glass. Even without the beverages, whether it be a cocktail shaker, decanter, or pilsener glass, these are all items that give aesthetic pleasure—vessels that are inextricably tied to our culture, history and identity. Cheers!

"Quinac" advertisement (c.1948). *Courtesy of David C. Cooper.*

Part I
Cocktail Shakers

When one mentions vintage barware, the first thing that unerringly leaps to mind is the cocktail shaker. There is something about glass and an iced beverage that makes the combination irresistable. Amelia Leavitt Hill wrote in her 1949 *Table Setting* book that "Cocktail shakers in glass are usually more satisfactory than those in metal, since they show the amount they hold at a glance. Moreover, they do not become battered from the ice within them as metal shakers are apt to do."

Paden City #902 crystal cocktail shaker, rooster stopper, 3-piece, cut criss-cross and dots, $95; cocktail glasses, $20 each. *Author's collection.*

Paden City #902 crystal cocktail shaker, rooster stopper, 3-piece, "Gazebo" etch, 13", $175. *Courtesy of David C. Cooper.*

Heisey #4225 "Cobel" (1932-57) crystal cocktail shaker, "Horse Head" top (scarce), 15", 1 quart, $175. Named for the designer Ray C. Cobel, head of Heisey's mold shop. Patent #1,966,611 granted July 17th, 1934.

Heisey #4225 "Cobel" (1932-57) crystal cocktail shaker, showing horse head and rooster head tops, 15", 1 quart, $175 each. Other figural cocktail shaker tops were a ram's head and girl's head ($150+ for these tops alone). The rooster is the most frequently seen of the four figures.

Cambridge #P101 "Pristine" crystal cocktail shaker, ball finial, 48 oz., 12": "Lattice" cut, $155; #1041 Rosepoint (1935-54) etch, $225; undecorated, 12", $125. *Courtesy of David C. Cooper.*

Close-up of Cambridge #P101 "Pristine" crystal decanter lids. *Courtesy of David C. Cooper.*

Heisey #4225 "Cobel" (1932-57) crystal cocktail shaker, rooster head, 1 pint, 11-1/4", $115; 1 quart, with rattan handles, 14", $195. *Courtesy of David C. Cooper.*

Duncan Miller #11 crystal cocktail shaker, 16 oz., #640 "Laurel Wreath" rock crystal cutting, 10", $75; "Touraine" #503-1 liquor cocktail, 3-1/2 oz., 4-1/2", $25 each. *Courtesy of David C. Cooper.*

Cambridge #3400/157 crystal cocktail shaker, 12": #752 "Diane" etch, #5 chrome lid, $145; crystal cocktail shaker, "Portia" etch, $225. *Courtesy of David C. Cooper.*

Crystal cocktail shaker, Silver City silver overlay poppy, 10-1/2", $55. *Courtesy of David C. Cooper.*

Heisey #4225 "Cobel" (1932-57) crystal cocktail shaker, silver overlay rose, 12", $225. *Courtesy of David C. Cooper.*

Cambridge #3400/157 crystal cocktail shaker, #1041 "Rosepoint" etch (1935-54), 12-1/4", $225; #3121 saucer champagne, 6-3/4 oz., 6-1/2", $25. *Courtesy of David C. Cooper.*

Cambridge #3400/158 crystal cocktail shaker, applied handle, 10-1/2", $95. *Courtesy of David C. Cooper.*

Crystal cocktail shaker with diamond cut pattern, 10", $55. *Courtesy of David C. Cooper.*

West Virginia Glass Specialty crystal #741/10 "Long Feller" super-size cocktail shaker, 14", $110. *Courtesy of David C. Cooper.*

Crystal cocktail shaker, leaf cut, 10-1/2", $35; cocktail glasses, 3-1/4", $12 each. *Courtesy of Joan Gerber.*

Cambridge crystal cocktail shaker, "Chantilly" etch (1936-58), 13", $175; P101 "Pristine" cocktail shaker, ball finial, 48 oz., 12", $145; #3600 saucer champagne, 7 oz., 6", $20 each. *Courtesy of David C. Cooper.*

West Virginia Specialty crystal cocktail shaker, "Mallard Ducks" Rockwell silver overlay, 10-1/4", $125; pitcher, 9-1/4", $65. *Courtesy of David C. Cooper.*

Duncan Miller #5200 crystal cocktail shaker, "Mallard Duck Design" silver intaglio etching (1940s), 11", $225; #115 "Canterbury" (1938-55) martini mixer, handled, 32 oz., 9-1/2", $225. *Courtesy of David C. Cooper.*

Duncan Miller #11 crystal cocktail shaker, #688 "Juno" rock crystal cutting, 10", $175. *Courtesy of David C. Cooper.*

Duncan Miller #5200 crystal cocktail shaker, "First Love" etch (1937), 11-1/4", $295; crystal #115 "Canterbury" (1938-55) crystal martini mixer with spoon, handled, 32 oz., 9-1/4", $275. *Courtesy of David C. Cooper.*

Duncan Miller #112 "Caribbean" (1936-55) crystal cocktail shaker, 33 oz., 12", $95. *Courtesy of David C. Cooper.*

Duncan Miller #5301 "Teardrop" (1936-55) crystal: cocktail mixer, 8", $175; saucer champagne, 5 oz., 5-1/4", $12. *Courtesy of David C. Cooper.*

Paden City #69 "Georgian" (c.1934) crystal cocktail shaker, 30 oz., 11", $55. Weatherman dubbed this "Aristocrat." *Courtesy of David C. Cooper.*

Paden City #215 "Glades" crystal cocktail shaker, floral cut, 11", $125. *Courtesy of David C. Cooper.*

Paden City #215 "Glades" crystal cocktail shaker, "Spring Orchard" etched, 11", $155. *Courtesy of David C. Cooper.*

Imperial-Heisey West Point shaker etch detail.

Imperial-Heisey #4225 "Cobel" (1932-57) crystal cocktail shaker, West Point etch "USMR MDCCII" (1803), 12-1/4", $125. *Courtesy of David C. Cooper.*

Heisey #4225 Cobel (1932-57) crystal cocktail shaker, signed Bach "Mallard Duck" cut (outside cutting firm), 11-3/4", $175. *Courtesy of David C. Cooper.*

Heisey "Mallard Duck" shaker detail.

WMF German crystal crackle glass cocktail shaker, 8", $145. WMF are the initials for the German glass producer Wurttembergische Metallwarenfabrik AG, Geislingen/Steige, Germany (1883-present). *Courtesy of David C. Cooper.*

Crystal cocktail shakers: English open square, 8-3/4", $75; Val St. Lambert, crisscross, 10-1/4", $175; Belgian paneled, 8-1/4", $75. *Courtesy of David C. Cooper.*

Crystal cocktail shaker, cut, 11-1/2", $45.
Courtesy of David C. Cooper.

Hazel-Atlas crystal cocktail shaker, "Pennsylvania" gold state shield, 9-1/4", $55; old fashioneds, 3-1/4", $12 each. *Courtesy of David C. Cooper.*

Indiana Glass "Cocktailor" (mid-1950s) crystal 7 piece cocktail set: cocktail shaker, 9-1/2"; cocktail tumblers, 2-1/2"; metal stirring spoon; set $75. *Courtesy of David C. Cooper.*

Indiana "Cocktailor" set in original box.

West Virginia Specialty recipe cocktail shakers: cobalt, 9", $125; crystal, 10-3/4", $75; ruby, 9", $115. *Courtesy of David C. Cooper.*

Duncan Miller #11 cocktail shakers: cobalt, 11-1/4", $145; ruby, 11", $145; green, 11", $125. *Courtesy of David C.*

Duncan Miller "Chanticleer" cocktail shakers, 16 oz.: cobalt, 6-1/2", $255; ruby, 6", $225. *Courtesy of Jeff & Mary Czech.*

Hazel-Atlas cobalt cocktail shakers: "Windmill," 9-1/2", $45; "Ships," 9-3/4", $65. *Author's collection.*

Hazel-Atlas cobalt cocktail shaker "Fishes", 10-1/2", $125; juice tumbler, water tumbler, $15 each. *Courtesy of Valerie & Bill McCormack.*

Hazel-Atlas cobalt cocktail shakers, with recipes, 10-1/2", $85; 9-1/2", $75. *Courtesy of Valerie & Bill McCormack.*

Cobalt cocktail shaker, ribbed, 10-3/4", $75; cocktail glasses with metal foot, 4-1/2", $15 each. *Courtesy of Valerie & Bill McCormack.*

MacBeth-Evans cocktail shakers: cobalt, 11", $75; ruby, 10-1/2" $85. *Courtesy of David C. Cooper.*

Duncan Miller #11 ruby cocktail shaker, 11", $95; "Cathay" cocktail glasses, 4", $35 each. *Courtesy of David C. Cooper.*

West Virginia Specialty ruby cocktail shaker with platinum decoration, 11", $95. *Courtesy of Jeff & Mary Czech.*

Fenton "Georgian" (c.1935) ruby cocktail shaker, silver strainer top missing, 24 oz., 7-1/2", $125; amberina footed cordial, 1 oz., $25. Originally marketed as "Agua Caliente" (Spanish for "Hot Water")—"Styled in the spirit of today, but suggesting the charm of Early American days." *Courtesy of Donna Hatch.*

Ruby cocktail shaker, 9-3/4", $95. *Courtesy of David C. Cooper.*

Duncan Miller ruby martini mixer, 8-1/2", $155; ruby #55 shot glasses, 2", $35 each. David C. Cooper.

New Martinsville #37 "Moondrops" (1932-40) amber cocktail shaker, 6-1/2", $125; footed tumblers, 9 oz., 4-3/4", $15 each. *Courtesy of David C. Cooper.*

Cambridge #3400/159 amber cocktail shaker, handled, 11", $125. *Courtesy of Valerie & Bill McCormack.*

Westmoreland #1707 amber cocktail shaker, 11", $75. *Courtesy of Francois Houle.*

West Virginia Specialty "Barbell" (c.1937) amber cocktail shaker, 13", $125. *Courtesy of Valerie & Bill McCormack.*

Crystal recipe cocktail mixer, 6", $20. *Courtesy of Patricia Drumright.*

Reverse of recipe shaker.

Crystal "Boston" shakers, 2-part with stainless steel cup, 6", $20 each. *Courtesy of Hampton's Antiques.*

Paden City #156 "Speakeasy" (c.1928) emerald green cocktail shaker, 9", $55. "Speakeasy" was Hazel Marie Weatherman's name for this cocktail.

Heisey #4225 "Cobel" Moongleam (green) cocktail shaker, 2 quart, 14", $550. *Courtesy of Russ Barker.*

Hocking green cocktail shaker, with reversible reamer top, grape cut, 10", $75. *Courtesy of Valerie & Bill McCormack.*

Hocking green cocktail shaker, 11-1/2", $55. *Courtesy of Jeff & Mary Czech.*

Hazel-Atlas #G-386 (c.1929) green cocktail shaker, with measurements, 8", $65. *Courtesy of Jeff & Mary Czech.*

Czechoslovakian forest green boot cocktail shaker, brass rim marked "Made in Czechoslovakia," 12", $350. *Author's collection.*

Green cocktail shaker, with ground glass stopper, 8", $85.

Duncan Miller "Chanticleer" (1920s-30s) cocktail shakers, 16 oz., 6-1/2": amber $125; green $475; green whiskey, 3 oz., 3", $45. *Courtesy of Jeff & Mary Czech.*

Morgantown #1 "Cadenza" (c.1923) #2402 vaseline cocktail shaker, with brass lid, 11", $255. *Courtesy of David C. Cooper.*

Duncan Miller #500 crystal "Nautical" cocktail shaker, with cobalt base, 30 oz., 11", $195. *Courtesy of David C. Cooper.*

Crystal shaker with cobalt foot, 9-1/2", $155. *Courtesy of David C. Cooper.*

West Virginia Glass Specialty crystal and frosted "Barbell" cocktail shaker, with 8-pointed star cut, 12", $95. *Courtesy of Valerie & Bill McCormack.*

Duncan Miller #11 crystal frosted cocktail shaker, 11-1/4", $135. *Courtesy of David C. Cooper.*

Duncan Miller "Chanticleer" crystal frosted cocktail shakers, 32 oz., 10-3/4", $155; 16 oz., 9-1/4", $125; whiskeys, 3 oz., 3", $20 each. *Courtesy of David C. Cooper.*

Crystal recipe cocktail shaker, 10", $35.
Courtesy of Hampton's Antiques.

Crystal cocktail shaker, black dots, 9", $35; black, yellow, and pink dot tumblers, 3", $5 each. *Courtesy of Leslie Hiscoe.*

Hocking crystal cocktail shaker, flags decoration, 10", $35. *Author's collection.*

Hocking "Rings" crystal cocktail shaker, red/orange/yellow/black rings, 11", $45. *Author's collection.*

Hocking "Pink Elephant" crystal cocktail shaker, 10-1/4", $65; tumbler, 3-1/4", $10. *Courtesy of Jeff & Mary Czech.*

Crystal recipe cocktail shaker, 10-1/2", $45. *Courtesy of David C. Cooper.*

Hocking crystal cocktail shaker, floral decoration, 10-1/2", $35. *Author's collection.*

Hazel Atlas "Polar Bear" crystal cocktail shaker, 10-1/2", $75; tumblers, 3", $12 each. *Courtesy of Valerie & Bill McCormack.*

Crystal cocktail shaker, diamond pattern, red lid, 9-1/2", $35; green lid, 11", $25. *Courtesy of Valerie & Bill McCormack.*

MacBeth-Evans crystal and frosted cocktail shaker, with gold trim, 11", $55; tumblers, 3", $12 each. *Courtesy of David C. Cooper.*

Federal crystal cocktail shaker with silver dots, 10-1/2", $35; tumbler, 3-1/2", $8; old fashioned tumbler, 3-1/4", $10. *Author's collection.*

West Virginia Glass Specialty crystal and frosted cocktail shaker, with platinum trim, 11", $35. *Author's collection.*

Part II

Decanters & Pitchers

Go figure! Even through the 1920s, the New Martinsville Glass Company—like many other glass manufacturers—brazenly advertised many styles of "Liquor Sets" for sale. In 1928, they had the audacity to market their Volstead Pup decanter. Andrew J. Volstead was the Congressman whose name is on the 1919 Volstead act that under the 18th Amendment banned all alcoholic beverages. By the late 1920s and early '30s the writing was on the wall. The "Great Experiment" of Prohibition had been a bust. When Prohibition was formally declared over on 5 December, 1933, all the glass companies were already in production with a multitude of new accoutrements for the merry imbibers who could now, after some fifteen years, drink legally.

Whatever terms various glass companies used to name their stoppered bottles, be it decanter, bar bottle, liquor set, or wine & brandy set, there is a surprisingly wide variety of forms and styles. A fine study of glass types and decorating styles could be undertaken by looking solely at decanters. The items illustrated in this chapter run the gamut of glass colors, types, and decoration—ruby, cobalt, black, crystal, amber, smoke, green, purple, yellow, black, jadite, opalescent, silver overlay, frosted, enameled, cut, etched, ruby stained, pinched, and in metal frames. Imaginative decanters such as the McKee Glass Company "Jolly Golfer" and "Lifesaver" are keenly sought after by many collectors.

Decanters

Paden City #991 "Penny Line" (1930s-1951) ruby decanter with crystal stopper, 22 oz., 10-3/4", $100; whiskey, 2-3/4", $30 each. *Courtesy of Jeff & Mary Czech.*

Paden City #991 "Penny Line" (1930s-1951) ruby decanter with ruby stopper, silver overlay, 22 oz., 10-3/4", $135; cordial, 3-1/4", $20 each. *Courtesy of Jeff & Mary Czech.*

Red decanter with stopper, 11", $75; footed cordials, $15 each. *Courtesy of Jeff & Mary Czech.*

Fenton #1934 (1934-38) ruby liquor decanter, platinum trim, with floral stopper, 9", $225. Originally sold with a floral embossed tray and whiskey goblets. *Courtesy of Donna Hatch.*

New Martinsville #42 "Radiance" (1936-44) ruby decanter with stopper, handled, 16 oz., 8-1/2", $225; cordials, 1 oz., 2-1/2", $20 each.

Paden City #214 ruby decanter, cordial tilt, with stopper, silver overlay, 10", $35. *Doris McMullen.*

New Martinsville "Novelty Roly Poly Whiskey" (1934) ruby decanter with fan-shaped stopper, handled, 12 oz., 7-1/2", $75. "Just right for Brandy or cordials." *February 1934 Crockery and Glass Journal. Courtesy of Jeff & Mary Czech.*

Paden City #215-1/2 ruby tilt cordial decanter with stopper, poppy silver overlay decoration marked "Sterling," 6-3/4", $55. *Author's collection.*

New Martinsville #15 (c.1935) ruby decanter with crystal stopper, 11-1/2", $75; cocktail glasses, 4-1/4", $15 each. *Author's collection.*

Cambridge "Mt. Vernon" Carmen (red) decanter with stopper, 40 oz., $100; footed tumblers, 3 oz., 2-1/2", $20 each. *Courtesy of Jeff & Mary Czech.*

McKee red pinch decanter with stopper, 9-1/2", $75; McKee black pinch decanter with stopper, $85; Cambridge #1070 ruby pinch decanter with stopper, 36 oz., 10-1/2", $85. *Author's collection.*

Viking #1821 "Bullseye" (1944-70) ruby decanter with stopper, 11", $55. From Yesteryear line.

Cambridge #1070 ebony pinch decanter with stopper, silver overlay "Scotch," 36 oz., 10-1/2", $125. *Author's collection.*

Ruby decanter with stopper, 9-1/4", $55.

Fenton #1667 CR opalescent cranberry wine bottle with stopper, "New World" line (1953-63), 14-1/2", $225; QVC Heritage green opalescent Wine Bottle, 14-1/2", $95. QVC (Quality, Value & Convenience) bought mainly Fenton glass items specially created for their live television shows. Typically between 250 and 1000 pieces were made for each broadcast and would sell out within minutes.

European ruby flashed decanter and stopper, floral cut, 10-1/2", $125. *Courtesy of Wayne Boyd.*

"Ring Of Rings" cobalt decanter with stopper, 10", $35; tumbler, 2-3/4", $8. Attributed to Hazel-Atlas. *Author's collection.*

Imperial #451 "Shaeffer" cobalt decanter with jigger stopper, 10-1/4", $225; tumblers, 5 oz., 3", $15 each. Named by the pioneering glass researcher Hazel Marie Weatherman. *Courtesy of Jeff & Mary Czech.*

Fostoria #2494 (1934-40) Regal blue cordial bottle, $65; #4024 cordials, $25 each.

Thos. Webb & Sons, England "Bristol" cobalt decanter with stopper, signed, in original box, 11", $155. *Author's collection.*

Imperial #56 "Provincial" turquoise blue decanter with stopper, 10-1/2", $75; saucer champagne, 4", $25; cordials, 2-3/4", $20 each. *Author's collection.*

Cambridge #3400/92 cobalt ball shape decanter with stopper, 32 oz., in Farber Brothers chrome frame, 7", $100; #3400/92 cobalt tumbler, 2-1/2 oz., $15 each. *Author's collection.*

Imperial "Mt. Vernon" Antique Blue decanter with stopper, gold decoration, 11-3/4", $55; cocktail glasses, 5", $10 each. *Courtesy of David C. Cooper.*

Czechoslovakian blue decanter with stopper, floral silver overlay, 9-1/2", $55; tumblers, 2-1/4", $8 each. *Courtesy of Francois Houle.*

Crystal and metal lighthouse decanter, 10-3/4", $75. Eastern European (note the hammer and sickle), plays "How Dry Am I" when lifted. *Courtesy of Hampton's Antiques.*

Tiara #10047 "Jolly Mountaineer" (1980) blue frosted decanter with tumbler lid, 37 oz., 10-1/4", $75. Tiara was the home party division of the Indiana Glass Company. Items were created from old moulds from Duncan Miller, Federal, Fostoria, and Imperial. To our eye, this decanter certainly looks to be a spitting image of that great comedian and legendary imbiber, W. C. Fields.

Smoke decanter, jigger stopper, ground pontil, 6-1/4", $55; tumbler, 2-3/4", $8. *Author's collection.*

Hocking #300 "Banded Rings" (1927-33) crystal decanter with stopper, black/orange/yellow/red rings, 11-1/2", $35; whiskey, 1-1/2 oz., 2-1/4", $8 each. *Author's collection.*

Czechoslovakian yellow decanter with stopper, deco, 9", $65; tumblers, 1-1/2", $10 each. *Author's collection.*

New Martinsville #38 "Hostmaster" bar bottle with stopper, 13", $75; old fashioned, 3-1/4", $20 each; muddlers, 5-1/2", $10 each. Advertised in 1934: "Our New Repeal Set Is a Wow!" *Courtesy of Jeff & Mary Czech.*

New Martinsville #15 (c.1935) amber decanter with clear fan-shaped stopper, 11-1/2", $75; tray, 10-1/4", $35; cocktail, 4-1/4", $15 each. *Author's collection.*

Ribbed amber decanter with stopper, $55. *Author's collection.*

New Martinsville #37 "Moondrops" amber decanter with fan-shaped stopper, "Roberto" etch, 13", $95; footed tumbler, 3 oz., 3-1/2", $18 each. *Courtesy of Jeff & Mary Czech.*

Duncan Miller #118 "Hobnail" amber decanter with stopper, 12 oz., 8-1/2", $125; 2 oz. whiskey, 2-1/4", $25 each. *Courtesy of David C. Cooper.*

Cambridge #3400 (c.1940) amber decanter with stopper, faceted stopper, Farber Brothers chrome base, 24 oz., 12-1/4", $75; Cambridge #5791 amber decanter with stopper, Farber Brothers chrome base, 14 oz., 11-1/2", $95. Glass inserts were available in amber, amethyst, forest green, Carmen, ebony, and Royal blue. Each set was sold with six cordials of either a matching color or a rainbow assortment. *Courtesy of Jeff & Mary Czech.*

Amber decanter with stopper, deco, 10-1/4", $45. *Author's collection.*

Czechoslovakian amber/green decanter with stopper, geometric cut, 8", $55; footed tumblers, $10 each. *Courtesy of Francois Houle.*

Cambridge topaz (vaseline) decanter in Century Silver Company metal frame, 11", $125. *Courtesy of Valerie & Bill McCormack.*

Czechoslovakian green/ black decanter and stopper, 11", $55; footed tumblers, 2-3/4", $12 each. *Author's collection.*

Cambridge #1321 decanters with stoppers, 28 oz., 11": cobalt $95, amber $35, amethyst $45. *Courtesy of David C. Cooper and Jeff & Mary Czech.*

Cambridge #1321 amethyst decanter with stopper, 11", $75; #7966 sherry, 2 oz., 5-1/4", $12 each. *Author's collection.*

Cambridge #3400/92 ball-shape decanter with stopper, 32 oz.: amber $45; amethyst $55. *Author's collection.*

French amber duck decanter, 6"; handled tray, 5-1/2"; multicolor tumblers, 2-1/4". Set $350.

Czechoslovakian green decanter with stopper, deco, 8", $75; tumblers, 2-1/2", $12 each. *Courtesy of Steve Lindsay.*

Czechoslovakian green decanter with stopper, silver overlay of Venetian scenes, 8-3/4", $35; tumblers, 2-1/4", $8 each. *Author's collection.*

Consolidated "Catalonian" green decanter, 6-1/4", $250; tray, 10-1/2", $125; tumblers, 2-3/4", $35 each. *Courtesy of Francois Houle.*

Hocking #G102 green pinch decanter with stopper, 10", $55. *Author's collection.*

McKee "Life Saver" green decanter with stopper, 12-1/2", $275. A 1927 ad announced "A New Decanter Set that is useful for Many Occasions...Sold in the following transparent colors: rose pink, green, blue, amber, canary or crystal. Special at $5.00 each List." *Courtesy of Francois Houle.*

Green decanter, "Laurel Wreath" etch, 28 oz., 11", $75. *Courtesy of David C. Cooper.*

Hocking "Cameo" (1930-34) decanter with stopper, 10", $225; green decanter with stopper, deco, 10", $55. Note that both of these decanters were fitted with the same stopper, which many savvy collectors swiped from the cheaper deco decanter to fit the more elusive and expensive Cameo decanter.

Cambridge #3400/92 Crown Tuscan ball-shape decanter with stopper, 32 oz., 7", $550. *Courtesy of Jeff & Mary Czech.*

McKee "Jolly Golfer" (1926) green decanter, 11-1/2", $475; tumbler with hat/lid, 2-3/4", $75; frosted crystal tumbler, 2-3/4", $45. The caption on an early ad reads "FORE! here's the Jolly Golfer by Tony Sarg and The McKee Glass Co."

Czechoslovakian pink decanter, 8-1/2", $55; tumbler, 2-1/4", $12 each. *Courtesy of Francois Houle.*

Cambridge emerald green cat decanter, 8-1/4", $125; New Martinsville #1926 "Volstead Pup" rose (pink) decanter, 9", $55; shot glass, $20. "You'll be surprised at what he has under his hat in the way of new specialties" (from the "Pottery, Glass and Brass Salesman"). Around the same time, New Martinsville also produced a "Nice Kitty" liquor set. Buyers could mix and match "3 dozen to a barrel—assorted dogs and cats." *Courtesy of Jeff & Mary Czech.*

Fenton "An American Legacy Collection" Colonial green decanter with stopper, 13", $95; Candleglow yellow decanter with stopper, 12-1/4", $75. *Courtesy of Donna Hatch.*

Czechoslovakian yellow decanter with stopper, deco, 8", $85; tumbler, 2", $20 each. *Courtesy of Francois Houle.*

Duncan Miller #56 "Gordon" crystal decanter with stopper, "Spider Web" cut, 32 oz., 10-1/2", $95; martini, 5-1/4", $20; #55 whiskey, 1-1/2 oz., 2", $25 each. *Courtesy of David C. Cooper.*

Paden City "Drape" crystal decanter, applied handle, 7", $75; footed tumbler, 2-1/2", $20 each. *Courtesy of Jeff & Mary Czech.*

Paden City #211 "Spire" crystal decanter with stopper, four-lobed, "Spring Orchard" etch, 10-1/2", $75; cocktail glasses, 4", $25 each. *Courtesy of Russ Barker.*

Paden City #211 "Spire" crystal demi-decanter, handled, four-lobed, "Spring Orchard" etch, $75; cocktail glasses, 4", $25 each.

Paden City #215-1/2 crystal tilt handled cordial decanter with stopper, rose cut, 6-1/4", $45; #215 crystal decanter with stopper, Cornflower-type cut (possibly R.G. Sherriff), 9", $35. *Courtesy of Russ Barker.*

Paden City #215 crystal decanter with stopper, etched scotch, 9", $75.

Duncan Miller #640 "Laurel Wreath" rock crystal cutting: #5200 crystal decanter with stopper, 32 oz., 9-1/4", $85; #503 "Touraine" crystal cocktail glasses, $25 each. "Rock Crystal Cuttings. Where a glistening, clear crystal cutting is desired, the gray finish is removed by dipping the glass into a bath of acid." (from 1943 Duncan Miller catalogue). *Courtesy of David C. Cooper.*

Duncan Miller #55 "Gordon" Ruby & Crystal decanter with stopper, 9-1/2", $95; "Dover" cocktail glass, 4-1/2", $35. *Courtesy of David C. Cooper.*

Crystal decanter with stopper, from Finland, pebble finish, 7-1/2", $75; shot glass, 2-1/4", $12 each. *Courtesy of Francois Houle.*

Crystal decanter with stopper, 12-1/4", $45. *Author's collection.*

Frosted crystal decanter and shot glasses, silver overlay sailboat, 8". Set $75. *Author's collection.*

Hazel-Atlas frosted crystal Scotch decanter with stopper, marked "HA," 9", $35. *Author's collection.*

Morgantown #1933 LMX Ice ("a semi-opaque white that bears out its name") "El Mexicano" (1933) decanter with stopper, made to look like an ice cube, 8-1/2", $225. *Courtesy of Jeff & Mary Czech.*

Hocking "Cameo" (1930-34) crystal decanter with stopper, 10-1/2", $275.

George Duncan #800 (c.1890) crystal decanter with hand cut stopper, gold and hand-painted cornflowers, 12", $155; "Mitchell" cordial, 4", $35 each; tray with star center, 10-1/2", $125. *Courtesy of David C. Cooper.*

Duncan Miller #30 "Pall Mall" decanter with stopper, "Language of Flowers" etch, 11", $125; "Victory" stems, 4-3/4", $25 each. *Courtesy of David C. Cooper.*

George Duncan crystal #1 (c.1884) decanter with stopper, cut #15, 11-1/2", $155. *Courtesy of David C. Cooper.*

Heisey #351 "Priscilla" (1904-30) crystal decanter with stopper, 1 quart, 11", $125. *Courtesy of David C. Cooper.*

Fostoria #319 (1934-37) crystal bar bottle with stopper, silhouette of horse and carriage, 11", $45. *Author's collection.*

Pitchers

McKee jug (c.1935) with metal frame handle and hinged lid, 9-3/4": ruby, $125; cobalt, $155. One of these pitchers in crystal can be seen in vintage pictures of the bar at the famous Stork Club in New York City. *Courtesy of Valerie & Bill McCormack.*

West Virginia Specialty crystal martini pitcher with stir stick, silver overlay "Flying Ducks," 10", $95. *Courtesy of Roger LeBlanc.*

Hazelware "The Magic Hour 4 pc. Cocktail Set" Moroccan Amethyst cocktail glasses, 2-1/2", $10 each; cocktail mixer, 6-1/4", $30; metal stir spoon, $10. *Author's collection.*

West Virginia Specialty (c.1950) crystal martini recipe pitchers, 6-1/2", $25; 8-1/2", $35. *Courtesy of David C. Cooper.*

West Virginia Specialty (c.1950) crystal martini pitcher, 11", $45; cocktail tumbler, 4-1/2 oz., 3-1/4", $8 each; stir stick, $10. *Courtesy of David C. Cooper.*

Morgantown #2009 "Milano" crystal martini mixer, from the Décor line, 11", $75; old fashioned tumblers, 3-3/4", $25 each. *Courtesy of David C. Cooper.*

White cocktail pitcher with rattan, 9-3/4", $45; cocktail glasses, 3", $10 each. *Courtesy of Valerie & Bill McCormack.*

Heisey "Coronation" (c.1950) crystal pitcher with "Mallard Duck" cutting, 8-1/4", $75. *Courtesy of David C. Cooper.*

West Virginia Glass Specialty (c.1960) crystal martini pitcher, with "Mallard Duck" etch by Lotus Glass Company, 10 1/2", $75; cocktail glass, 3-1/2", $15 each. *Courtesy of David C. Cooper.*

West Virginia Glass Specialty crystal pitcher, green applied handle, 7-1/2", $35. *Courtesy of David C. Cooper.*

Fenton #1700 "Lincoln Inn" (1928-40) crystal pitcher, 14-1/4", $85; highball, 12 oz., 7-1/4", $25; tumbler, 9 oz., 5-1/4", $12. *Courtesy of Kathy McCarney.*

"Frigid Tube" crystal pitcher, 11-3/4", $55. "Fill tube with either ice cubes or crushed ice replacing plastic cap. Place tube in freezer compartment of refrigerator…When ready to serve cold drinks without diluting, place ice filled tube into pitcher." *Courtesy of Russ Barker.*

Fry "Milkmaid" crystal pitcher, 10", $450; tumbler, 5-1/2", $75.
Courtesy of Valerie & Bill McCormack.

Fry "Foval" (c.1930) pitcher, radio wave pattern, blue applied handle, 9-1/4", $450. *Courtesy of Valerie & Bill McCormack.*

Part III

Beverage Dispensers, Samovars & Punch Sets

For quite some time, a mystery among collectors has been "Who made the various samovars that are found?" Some have sagely suggested a European connection. However, recent research has uncovered the fact that the glass molds for most of the typically seen samovars were owned by the Century Silver Company of New York. Century Silver commissioned both Cambridge Glass and Paden City Glass companies to make the glass inserts for their metal samovar frames. Production of these samovars began in the 1920s.

Paden City workers recalled making samovars as dispensers for coffee or other liquid refreshments for restaurants, soda fountains or bars. Papers still exist from the Cambridge Glass company listing items made for private mold owners. Although many of the notations are sketchy at best, it is thought that samovars were also referred to as "whiskey percolators." That sure would have been one awfully healthy supply of whiskey! At the time of this writing (spring 2005), a splendid assortment of several dozen samovars is on display at the Cambridge Glass Musuem in Cambridge, Ohio.

There are two main theories about the origin of the Tom & Jerry. Its earliest appearance seems to come in a lengthily entitled book *Life in London; or, The Day and Night Scenes of Jerry Hawthorn, Esq., and his elegant friend, Corinithian Tom* (1821) by Pierce Egan. In this volume, Egan named a version of egg nog the "Tom & Jerry." The second and most widely held belief is that the incomparable Professor Jerry Thomas, dubbed the father of all bartenders, created the "Tom & Jerry." While a bartender at the Occidental Hotel in San Francisco in the 1860s, he published the first book of drink recipes entitled *How to Mix Drinks or The Bon Vivant's Companion*. In this book was Thomas' concoction for a Tom & Jerry that many believe he invented in the 1850s. He most certainly did the most to publicize this and many other alcoholic beverages as he took his travelling bartending show on the road throughout North America and Europe.

Here is a Tom & Jerry recipe (to serve twelve): Separate twelve fresh eggs, beat yolks until smooth, add three tablespoons of sugar and two teaspoons of grated nutmeg. Add six jiggers of Jamaica rum, beat whites until stiff and whip into the mixture, add three jiggers brandy. Divide concoction into twelve mugs and fill with hot water or hot milk.

Beverage Dispensers

"Hires" milk glass beverage dispenser, hand painted, copper stand, 11", $300. *Courtesy of Valerie & Bill McCormack.*

Crystal beverage dispenser, pictured upside down, deco, metal vise stand, 16-1/2", $250. *Courtesy of Valerie & Bill McCormack.*

"Nu Grape" crystal beverage dispenser, fired-on green base, unique 3-part assembly, deco bottom portion, top is reminiscent of gallon jugs from the 1920s-1940s, 16-1/2", $350. *Courtesy of Valerie & Bill McCormack.*

"Iced Nestea" crystal beverage dispenser, black base and lid, "Tea on the Rocks," 24", $350. *Courtesy of Valerie & Bill McCormack.*

Crystal "Orange Crush" beverage dispenser, black base, agitator, orange lettering, 13-3/4", $350. *Courtesy of Valerie & Bill McCormack.*

Vintage "Lemon Crush" label. *Author's collection.*

Crystal beverage dispenser, deco, black base, 14", $350. *Courtesy of Valerie & Bill McCormack.*

"Grape Ola" crystal beverage dispenser, milk glass base, 10-3/4", $350. *Courtesy of Valerie & Bill McCormack.*

"Putnams Wine" crystal beverage dispenser, deco, milk glass base, 10-1/2", $300. *Courtesy of Valerie & Bill McCormack.*

"Moxie" crystal beverage dispenser, milk glass base, 9-1/2", $350. *Courtesy of Valerie & Bill McCormack.*

"Ice Tea" crystal beverage dispenser, "Quid Decus Verumatue" coat of arms, aluminum base, lemon wedge finial, 24", $300. *Courtesy of Valerie & Bill McCormack.*

McKee No. 9 crystal beverage dispenser, inner jar to keep the beverage separate from the ice, 19-1/2", $275. In their ad for McKee's No. 1 Sanitary Beverage Cooler and Dispenser, it was noted to be "A Silent Salesman – Neat – Sanitary – Displays Beverage to best advantage." *Courtesy of Valerie & Bill McCormack.*

Crystal beverage dispenser with clambroth base, deco red Bakelite finial, 12", $300. *Courtesy of Valerie & Bill McCormack.*

"Cali Orange" frosted crystal beverage dispenser, fired-on green base, 14-3/4", $300. *Courtesy of Valerie & Bill McCormack.*

Crystal beverage dispenser, fired-on green base, agitator, 14", $300. *Courtesy of Valerie & Bill McCormack.*

"Lash's Juice" green beverage dispenser, black base, green finial, 12-1/2", $450. *Courtesy of Valerie & Bill McCormack.*

Paden City "Fowler's Cherry Smash" red beverage dispenser, "Cherry Blended with other Fruit Flavors," 8-1/2", $400. *Courtesy of Valerie & Bill McCormack.*

"Canada Dry" frosted crystal beverage dispenser, "Ice Cold 5¢," green lettering, metal lid, 10", $275. *Courtesy of Valerie & Bill McCormack.*

"Mission Orange" cardboard advertising fan, 11-1/4" x 7-1/2". $35. *Courtesy of Valerie & Bill McCormack.*

Orange "Nesbitt's" pink beverage dispenser, pink base, "California Orange Juice – it's healthful," 12", $350. *Courtesy of Valerie & Bill McCormack.*

"Mission" beverage dispensers, "Real Fruit Juice," metal foot and lid, pink orange juice, 12-1/2", $275; green grapefruit juice, $300. *Courtesy of Valerie & Bill McCormack.*

"Mission" pink beverage dispenser, black base, orange juice, lid missing, 12-3/4", $350. *Courtesy of Valerie & Bill McCormack.*

Samovars

Cambridge/Paden City frosted blue samovar, bird handles, metal base and lid, 15", $450. *Courtesy of Doris McMullen.*

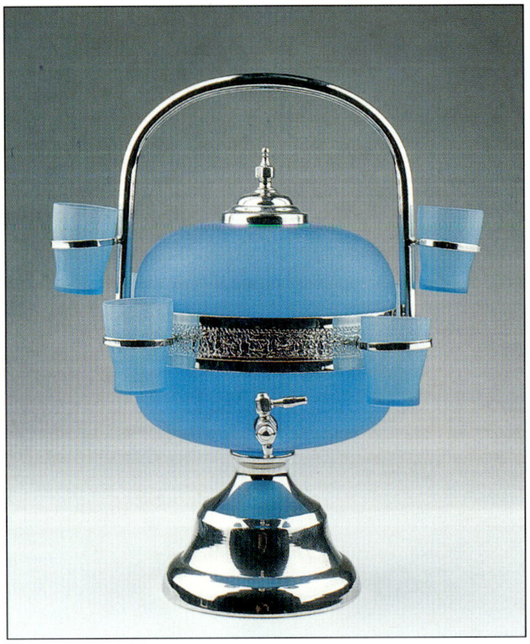

Frosted blue samovar, handled, metal base and lid, tumblers, re-silvered, 14-1/2", $450. *Courtesy of Francois Houle.*

Teal samovar, metal base and lid, 13", $400.
Courtesy of Valerie & Bill McCormack.

Cambridge dark blue samovar, etched, metal base and lid, 12-3/4", #1000 blown tumblers in metal bases, set $650. *Courtesy of Norma Brown.*

Cambridge/Paden City "Windmill" teal samovar, metal base and lid, 14-3/4", and 6 tumblers, 2-1/4", spiral optic, $350. *Courtesy of Kathy McCarney.*

Cambridge/Paden City "Windmill" amethyst samovar, metal base and lid, 14-3/4", and 4 tumblers, 2-1/4", spiral optic, $450.

Cambridge/Paden City amber samovar, 2-handled, 13-1/2", #1000 blown tumblers with metal bases, re-silvered, 5-1/2", set $450. *Courtesy of Francois Houle.*

Paden City, amber samovar, base missing (pictured complete on following page), sterling silver peacock decoration, 11-3/4", $275. *Courtesy of Valerie & Bill McCormack.*

Paden City green samovar, 2-handled, with green base, 15-1/2", $350. *Courtesy of Francois Houle.*

Cambridge/Paden City frosted green samovar, metal base and lid, bird handles, hand-painted floral, re-silvered, 15", $550. *Courtesy of Francois Houle.*

Cambridge/Paden City frosted crystal samovar, 4-footed metal base and lid, hand-painted floral decoration, 12-3/4", $325. *Courtesy of Doris McMullen.*

Crystal samovar, handled, metal base and lid, 14-1/2", $125. *Courtesy of Francois Houle.*

Punch Sets

McKee jade green Tom & Jerry set (c.1935), bowl, 4 quarts, 5"; 8 mugs, 6 oz., 3-1/2", black script lettering, set $375. *Courtesy of Valerie & Bill McCormack.*

McKee jade green Tom & Jerry set (c.1935), bowl, 4 quarts, 5"; 8 mugs, 6 oz., 3-1/2", black script lettering and trim, set $375. *Courtesy of Valerie & Bill McCormack.*

McKee jade green Tom & Jerry set (c.1935), bowl, 4 quarts, 5"; 8 mugs, 6 oz., 3-1/2", gold script lettering and trim, set $375. *Courtesy of Valerie & Bill McCormack.*

McKee black Tom & Jerry set (c.1935), bowl, 4 quarts, 5"; 8 mugs, 6 oz., 3-1/2", white script lettering, set $325. *Courtesy of Valerie & Bill McCormack.*

McKee French Ivory (custard) Tom & Jerry set (c.1935), bowl, 4 quarts, 5"; 8 mugs, 6 oz., 3-1/2", gold script lettering and trim, set $175. *Courtesy of Valerie & Bill McCormack.*

McKee French Ivory (custard) Tom & Jerry set (c.1935), bowl, 4 quarts, 5"; 8 mugs, 6 oz., 3-1/2", black script lettering, set $175. *Courtesy of Valerie & Bill McCormack.*

McKee White Opal "Dewdrop" Tom & Jerry set (c.1935), bowl, 4 quarts, 5"; 8 mugs, 6 oz., 3-1/2", red script lettering, set $155. *Courtesy of Valerie & Bill McCormack.*

McKee White Opal "Dewdrop" Tom & Jerry set (c.1935), bowl, 4 quarts, 5"; 8 mugs, 6 oz., 3-1/2", fired-on decal winter sleigh ride scene, set $195. *Courtesy of Valerie & Bill McCormack.*

McKee White Opal "Dewdrop" Tom & Jerry set (c.1935), bowl, 4 quarts, 5"; 8 mugs, 6 oz., 3-1/2", fired-on decal Christmas bells decoration, set $195. *Courtesy of Valerie & Bill McCormack.*

McKee White Opal "Dewdrop" Tom & Jerry set (c.1935), bowl, 4 quarts, 5"; 8 mugs, 6 oz., 4-3/4", saucers, 5-1/2", red snowflake decoration, set $155. *Courtesy of Valerie & Bill McCormack.*

Cambridge #1221 "Swan" crystal punch bowl with base, 13" high, 14" diameter, 10" wide; 8 punch cups, 3-1/2" high, 5 oz., set $1550.

Hazel Atlas "Royal Lace" (1934-41) amethyst toddy or hot apple cider set: cookie jar base, metal tray, lid, and ladle, 8 roly poly glasses, set $225. *Courtesy of Valerie & Bill McCormack.*

Hazel Atlas "Royal Lace" (1934-41) Ritz blue (cobalt) toddy or hot apple cider set: cookie jar base, metal tray, lid, and ladle, 8 roly poly glasses, set $325. *Courtesy of Valerie & Bill McCormack.*

Part IV
Ice Buckets & Tubs

There are two styles of ice containers illustrated in this chapter. The ice bucket typically measures approximately 6" in height and is affixed with a metal handle. The generally smaller ice tub measures around 3-1/2" in height and more often than not has tab handles molded out of glass.

By adding a cover to their ice buckets, companies created new items, as pictured for the Liberty Glass Company (see page 81)—Liberty's ice bucket turned into a cookie jar when given a lid. Note that traditional cookie jars generally do not have metal bails (half hoop handles), though the Fenton Glass Company's macaroon jars do have wicker handles. Cambridge "Tally Ho" ice buckets, outfitted with chromium plated handles, were converted into pretzel jars or cookie jars with the addition of a lid, the former which would also fit very nicely into our barware theme.

To complete their ice buckets glass companies fitted them with matching metal handles and tongs ordered from outside firms. There is quite a range of variety in these metal additions. M. W. Carr of West Somerville, Massachusetts, provided the metal tongs for the Westmoreland Glass Company amongst others. They promoted themselves as being "The largest manufacturer of ice tub handles, ice tongs, and strainers...polished nickel, polished silver or brush gold finishes." The best innovation for bails came with the introduction of the chromium plated handle. These handles last wonderfully, usually with absolutely no sign of corrosion a half century later. Occasionally, the same firms provided decorative perforated metal liners to keep the ice above the melted drippings.

Fostoria #2375 ice buckets, spiral optic, 6", amber $45; violet $85; rose (pink) $65; azure (blue) $95; green $55. *Courtesy of Patrick Doherty.*

Heisey #467 "Tally Ho" ice buckets, 5-3/4", amber $55; green $85; crystal $45; cobalt $145. *Courtesy of Patrick Doherty.*

Cambridge ice buckets, "Apple Blossom" etch, 5-3/4", Gold Krystol (yellow) $195; crystal $95; amber $165. *Courtesy of Patrick Doherty.*

Cambridge ice buckets, #851 "Cleo" etch, 5-3/4", amber $85; Peach-blo (pink) $155; crystal $55; Moonlight blue $225; Emerald green $135. *Courtesy of Patrick Doherty.*

Cambridge #847 "Decagon" ice buckets, 5-3/4": Back row: amethyst $85, Ebony (black) $75, amethyst $85; Third row: Carmen (ruby) $155, Royal Blue (cobalt) $145; Second row: Emerald green $125, Peach-blo (pink) $125, amber $55, Forest green $65; Front row: Willow blue $65. *Courtesy of Patrick Doherty.*

Cambridge #1147 "Decagon" ice tubs, 3-1/4": Back row: Willow blue $55, amber $45; Front row: Peach-blo (pink), $55, Peach-blo $45, Emerald green $55. *Courtesy of Patrick Doherty.*

Fostoria ice buckets, #290 "Oak Leaf" etch (1928-31), 6": Rose (pink) $155; iridescent azure (blue) $225; crystal $85; green $155. *Courtesy of Patrick Doherty.*

Fostoria #2375 ice buckets, 6": rose (pink) "Pheasant Band" etch, $65; topaz (yellow) "Trojan" etch (1929-44), $85; amber #277 "Vernon" etch (1927-34), $75. *Courtesy of Patrick Doherty.*

Cambridge #845 "Oak Bucket," 6": Emerald green $65; amber $55; Peach-blo (pink) $65. *Courtesy of Patrick Doherty.*

Fostoria #2449 "Hermitage" (1932-45) ice tubs, 4-1/2": Wisteria $255; green $55; crystal $30; amber $35. *Courtesy of Patrick Doherty.*

Fostoria ice buckets, #2375 "Versailles" etch, 6": Rose (pink) $145; Azure (blue) $185; Topaz (yellow) $110; green $145. *Courtesy of Patrick Doherty.*

Heisey ice buckets: Sahara (yellow) #500 "Octagon" (1928-35), "Old Colony" etch, 4-1/2", $125; Moongleam (green) #1252 "Twist" (1928-37), 5-1/2", $185; Flamingo (pink) #500 "Octagon," 4-1/2", $175. *Courtesy of Patrick Doherty.*

Pink ice bucket, leaf cut pattern, 6" with 3-3/4" by 1-1/2" insert, $55. *Courtesy of Patrick Doherty.*

Cambridge Peach-blo (pink) #851 blank ice bucket, "Gloria" etch, 5-3/4", $165. *Courtesy of Patrick Doherty.*

Pink ice buckets, 6": with floral cut, $45; plain with ornate handle, $45; floral cut, $55. *Courtesy of Patrick Doherty.*

Cambridge Peach-blo (pink) ice buckets, "Rosalie" etch, one with gold encrustation, 5-3/4", $175 each. Note the considerable variation in size and detail in the etch on the two ice buckets. *Courtesy of Patrick Doherty.*

Duncan Miller #28 pink ice bucket, with cornflower cut possibly by Bobby Sherriff (a cutter for W. J. Hughes Corn Flower for 22 years before launching his own cutting shop in 1940, in Toronto, Canada), 6", $125. *Courtesy of Patrick Doherty.*

"Zigzag" ice buckets pink, 6", $35 each. Note the two very different shades of pink from different glass batches. *Courtesy of Patrick Doherty.*

Paden City #300 "Archaic" pink ice tub, tab handled, "Cupid" etch, 4-3/4", $350. *Courtesy of Jeff & Mary Czech.*

Jeannette "Hex Optic" (1928-32) pink ice bucket with metal handle, 5-1/2", $35. *Courtesy of Patrick Doherty.*

Cambridge #1121 ice bucket, "Chrysanthemum" etch, 6": Peach-blo (pink) $95; Emerald green $125; amber, $85. *Courtesy of Patrick Doherty.*

Cambridge #957 ice bucket, #695 etch, 6": Emerald green $95, amber $65, Peach-blo (pink) $95. *Courtesy of Patrick Doherty.*

Hocking "Block Optic" (1929-33) ice tubs, 3": green $55; pink $100; "Spiral" (1928-30) green ice tub, 3", $30. *Author's collection.*

Hocking "Cameo" (1930-34) ice tubs, 3": green $200; pink $650.

Westmoreland #1211 "Doreen" ice buckets, with floral cuts, 6": pink $55; green $45. *Courtesy of Patrick Doherty.*

Ice buckets, floral cuts, deco, 6": pink $45; green $55. *Courtesy of Patrick Doherty.*

Indiana "Tea Room" (1926-31) ice buckets 6-1/2": green $95, pink $95. *Courtesy of Patrick Doherty.*

Fenton #1502 "Diamond Optic" (1927-37) ice buckets, with floral cut, 6": green $75; Rose (pink) $75. *Courtesy of Patrick Doherty.*

Cambridge #1121 Peach-blo (pink) ice bucket, "Grape & Leaf" etched, 5-3/4", $95; Emerald green ice bucket, "Tulip" etched, 5-3/4", $85. *Courtesy of Patrick Doherty.*

Cambridge #3400/851 ice buckets, #752 "Diane" plate etch (1931-56), 5-3/4": Peach-blo (pink) $225, crystal $125. *Courtesy of Patrick Doherty.*

Liberty Works "American Pioneer" (1931-34) ice buckets, 6": green $75; crystal $45; pink $65. *Courtesy of Patrick Doherty.*

Cambridge #1851 Emerald green ice bucket, #739 etch, 5-3/4", $155; #957 Emerald green ice bucket, #E732 "Majestic" etch, 5-3/4", $125. *Courtesy of Patrick Doherty.*

Green ice bucket, pinched, 5-1/2", $45; Liberty Works #124/4 (c.1929) with floral cut, 6-1/4", $55. A 1929 Liberty ad announced "They are Crackerjacks." *Courtesy of Patrick Doherty.*

Liberty Works ice bucket with lid, 7-3/4", $95. Although often collected as a covered ice bucket, in a 1929 ad Liberty marketed this as a cookie jar, calling it "One of our smart fall presentations"; Paden City #191 "Party Line" #2 green ice bucket, 6", $65. *Courtesy of Patrick Doherty.*

Cambridge #1121 Emerald green ice bucket, #E733 "Peacock & Urn" etch, 6", $175. *Courtesy of Patrick Doherty.*

Fostoria #2375 "Fairfax" (1927-44) green ice buckets, 6": plain $45: floral rock crystal cut $55. *Courtesy of Patrick Doherty.*

Duncan Miller #40 "Spiral Flutes" (1924-30s) green ice tub, 3", $85. *Courtesy of Patrick Doherty.*

Central Glass Works aquamarine ice tub, rectangular, 4-1/4", $55. *Courtesy of Patrick Doherty.*

Central Glass Works amber ice tub, rectangular, etch #62, gold encrusted, $65; green ice tub, rectangular, gold band, 4-1/4", $65. *Courtesy of Patrick Doherty.*

Cambridge #847 Emerald green ice tub, "Rosalie" etch, 3-1/4", $100; #1122 amber ice tub, "Rosalie" etch, 3-1/4", $75. *Courtesy of Patrick Doherty.*

New Martinsville #38 "Hostmaster" amber ice tub (originally sold as a pretzel jar in 1933), 6", $95. *Courtesy Jeff & Mary Czech.*

Cambridge #847 "Decagon" Emerald green ice tub, #732 "Majestic" etch, 3-1/4", $95; Moonlight blue #733 "Peacock and Urn" ice tub, 3-1/4", $155. *Courtesy of Patrick Doherty.*

Cambridge #3550 "Caprice" (1936-57) ice buckets, 4 footed, 6": moonlight blue $175; crystal $55. *Courtesy of Patrick Doherty.*

Duncan Miller #115 "Canterbury" (1938-55) blue opalescent ice bucket, 6-1/2", $95. *Courtesy of Patrick Doherty.*

Hazel Atlas (c.1940) Ritz Blue (cobalt blue) ice tubs, 4-1/4": "Ships," $35; "Windmill," $25. *Courtesy of Patrick Doherty.*

Hazel Atlas Ritz Blue (cobalt blue) ice bowl with metal holder, 6-1/2", $45. *Courtesy of Lynda Edwards.*

Fostoria #2378 Azure (blue) ice bucket, #277 "Vernon" etch (1928-34), 6", $125. *Courtesy of Dale Basaraba.*

Light blue ice bucket, floral cut, 6", $75. *Courtesy of Patrick Doherty.*

Fostoria orchid (amethyst) #2378 ice bucket, #289 "Paradise" plate etch (1927-30), 6", $195. *Courtesy of Dale Basaraba.*

Fenton #1615 "Dolphins" (c.1929) amethyst ice jar, 6-1/2", $550. A rare item that was initially designed as a flower pot to which the dolphin handles were added. May have been sold originally with a liner/saucer.

Dell "Tulip" (c.1940) amethyst ice tub, 3", $55. *Author's collection.*

Paden City #215 "Glades" (1930s-40s) ruby ice bucket, with platinum trim, 4", $75; hour-glass cocktails, deco, 2-3/4", 3 oz., $25 each. *Courtesy of Jeff & Mary Czech.*

Hazel Atlas "Pink Elephant" crystal ice tub, 4-1/4", $45. *Author's collection.*

Bartlett-Collins "Scottie Dog" (c.1943) ice tub, 4-1/4", $35. *Author's collection.*

Hazel Atlas ice tubs, 4-1/4": "Circus," $25; "Red Maple Leaf," $25. *Author's collection.*

Cambridge crystal ice buckets, #1041 "Rosepoint" etch (1935-54), 5-3/4": Back row: 3400/#851, $165; 3900/#671, $185; Front row: #1402/52 "Tally-Ho", two styles, $195. *Courtesy of Patrick Doherty.*

Cambridge #3400/851 crystal ice buckets, 6": "Lucia" rock crystal cut, 6", $95; floral cut, $65; unknown rock crystal cut, $95. *Courtesy of Patrick Doherty.*

Cambridge crystal ice buckets, "Wildflower" plate etch (1940-58), 5-3/4": 3400/#851, $125; 3900/#671, $135. *Courtesy of Patrick Doherty.*

Cambridge #674 Martha crystal ice bucket, #671 "Chantilly" plate etch (1936-58): #671, 6": $175; "Pristine" crystal ice bucket, "Chantilly" plate etch, 4-3/4", $155; 3900/#671 crystal ice bucket, "Chantilly" plate etch, 5-3/4", $145. *Courtesy of Patrick Doherty.*

Cambridge #3400/851 crystal ice bucket, "Elaine" etch (1933-58), 5-3/4", $125; #1402/52 "Tally-Ho" crystal ice bucket, $155. *Courtesy of Patrick Doherty.*

Cambridge: #3400/851, "Portia" etch, 5-3/4", $95; #1402/52 "Tally Ho" crystal ice bucket, "Valencia" etch, 5-3/4", $95; #3400/851 crystal ice bucket, #748 "Lorna" etch, 5-3/4", $95. *Courtesy of Patrick Doherty.*

Fostoria crystal ice bucket, #2375 "June" etch, 6", $75. *Courtesy of Patrick Doherty.*

Cambridge #1402/52 "Tally-Ho" (1932-40s) crystal ice bucket, 5-3/4", $55; 3900/#671, 5-3/4", $55. *Courtesy of Patrick Doherty.*

Fenton #1611 "Georgian" (1931-42) crystal ice bucket, originally dubbed "Agua Caliente" when first marketed by Fenton in 1931, with floral cut, 5-3/4", $45; Duncan Miller #30 Pall Mall crystal ice bucket, "First Love" etch, 5-3/4", $100. *Courtesy of Patrick Doherty.*

Heisey #1503 "Crystolite" (1937-57) crystal ice bucket, 4-1/2", $100; Cambridge #3550 "Caprice" (1936-57) crystal ice bucket, 6", $85. *Courtesy of Patrick Doherty.*

Fostoria #2560 "Coronet" (1938-43) crystal ice bucket, 5", $55; Fostoria #2375 "Fairfax" crystal ice bucket, floral cut, 6", $45. *Courtesy of Patrick Doherty.*

Cambridge #1402 "Mt Vernon" crystal ice bucket ("Ice Pail with Chromium Plated Handle"), 5-1/2", $55; crystal ice bucket, "Diane" etch, 5-3/4", $95. *Courtesy of Patrick Doherty.*

Cambridge #3400/851 crystal ice buckets, 5-3/4": #751 "Cleo" etch (1921-45), $75; #744 "Apple Blossom" etch, $75. *Courtesy of Patrick Doherty.*

Blue and frosted crystal ice bucket, 6-1/4", $65; ship ice bucket, 6-1/4", $75. *Courtesy of Patrick Doherty.*

Heisey #1469 "Ridgleigh" crystal ice bucket, 3-3/4", $75; #1509 "Queen Ann" (1938-57) crystal ice cube bucket, dolphin feet, 6-3/4", $75. *Courtesy of Patrick Doherty.*

Fostoria #2443 Ebony (black) ice tub, 4-1/4", $55; Liberty Works "American Pioneer" (1931-34) crystal ice bucket, 6", $55; black ice bucket, 6", $55. *Courtesy of Patrick Doherty.*

Fostoria #2056 "American" crystal ice bucket, 3-3/4", $125; crystal ice bucket, note unique tilt handle/lid mechanism, possibly European, 5", $65. *Courtesy of Patrick Doherty.*

Fostoria #2378 crystal ice bucket, #290 "Oak Leaf" brocade (1927-31), 6", $95. *Courtesy of Patrick Doherty.*

Fostoria #2449 "Hermitage" crystal ice bucket, 4-1/2", $30. *Courtesy of Patrick Doherty.*

Duncan Miller #301 "Teardrop" crystal ice tub, floral cut, 6", $85. *Author's collection.*

Heisey #433 "Greek Key" (c.1920) crystal ice tub, 3-3/4", $125. *Courtesy of Russ Barker..*

Paden City #215 "Glades" crystal ice tub, ruby stained base, "Birds & Branches" etch, 4", $55. *Courtesy of Russ Barker..*

Paden City crystal ice bucket, #893 "Oriental Garden" etch, 5-1/2", $75. *Courtesy of Patrick Doherty.*

Jeannette "Dewdrop" (1953-56) ice buckets, 5-1/4": ruby $45; crystal $20. *Courtesy of Patrick Doherty.*

Part V
Beverage Glasses

In Heaven there is no beer, that is why we drink it here.

—Irish Saying

If we were to venture back 150 years or more, we'd find that drinking in many respects was an easier pastime. One would probably have a favorite mug for ale, a shot glass for whiskey, and a wine glass. By Victorian times, things were getting quite a bit fancier with more ostentatious displays of wealth leading to diverse shapes of beverage glasses. Jump forward to the Roaring Twenties when cocktails flowed and the costs of producing glassware plummeted, and my oh my was there ever a profusion of glasses to choose from!

One of the finest glass works of this era was the Morgantown Glass Company (1903-1975). In the late 1930s, they issued a primer for "Shapes and Sizes in Glassware for Beer, Wines and Liquors." No less than forty-seven different items were illustrated in this listing. Some barware was shown in two or more styles (cocktail glasses, for example). The following lengthy list, excerpted from the Morgantown publication, names only one of each type and further demonstrates the scope of the challenge regarding what to include in this volume:

Wines: cordial or cognac, claret or burgundy, port wine, champagne tumbler, hock or sauterne, champagne goblet, saucer champagne, hollow stem saucer champagne, American or tulip hollow stem saucer champagne, Roemer, brandy or pousse café, Rhine wine, port or sherry, sherry or madeira.

Beers or Ales: Hoffman house goblet, Fifth Avenue goblet, Milwaukee goblet, Hofbrau pilsener beer, New York goblet, split beer tumbler, Touraine goblet, pilsener beer, ale goblet, ale tumbler, St. Louis goblet.

Whiskies and Brandies: pony whisky, whisky tumbler, bar water or wash glass, old-fashioned cocktail, toddy, hot whisky, Tom and Jerry, hot whisky tumbler, Tom Collins, lemonade tumbler, seltzer Delmonico, fizz tumbler, hi ball tumbler, brandy and soda, crème de menthe, brandy inhaler, cocktail.

Stem Ware

Morgantown "Rooster Cocktails" cocktail glasses, "Harlequin Pastels": left to right: Shamrock Green, Topaz Mist, Champagne Pink, Smoke, Ruby, Copen Blue, Amethyst, Gloria Blue, 4", $40-$60 each. *Courtesy of Jeff & Mary Czech.*

Morgantown amber, amethyst, and forest green cocktail glasses, for Farber Brothers metalcraft (chromium plated, "non-tarnishing chrome"), 6", $15 each; 5-3/4", $15. *Author's collection.*

Morgantown "Jockey" cocktail glasses, crystal with topaz/amber stem, 6 oz., 4-3/4", $85 each. Made for Gulfstream Race Track, Hallandale Beach, Florida. *Courtesy of Jeff & Mary Czech.*

Morgantown "Top Hat" Copen Blue, Pink Champagne and Topaz Mist (Harlequin pastels) cocktail glasses made for the Knickerbocker Hotel, Chicago, Illinois, c.1940, 5-1/4", $85 each. *Author's collection.*

Morgantown #7720-1/2 "Pagoda" cocktail glasses, 4 oz., 4-3/4": Topaz Mist, $55; Violet, $55. *Courtesy of Francois Houle.*

Morgantown "Fischer" stemware, cased filament stems, 4-1/2": Spanish Red champagne, $55; Ritz Blue cocktail, $55 each. *Courtesy of Jeff & Mary Czech.*

Cambridge "Statuesque" (late-1950s) Carmen (ruby) crackle stems with crystal stems: champagne glass, 7-1/2", \$650; cocktail glass, 7-1/2", \$650; water goblet, \$750.

Cambridge "Statuesque" cocktails, 6-1/2": cobalt with crystal stem, \$195; crystal with ebony stem, \$175; amethyst with crystal stem, \$175.

Heisey #3389 "Duquesne" (1932-35) tangerine saucer champagnes, 5 oz., \$155 each. *Courtesy of Dale Basaraba.*

Paden City #991 "Penny Line" ruby cocktail glass, 4-1/4", \$20. Ruby cocktail glass, 4-1/2", \$15. *Author's collection.*

Bi-color pink and green cocktail glass, 4-3/4", $45. *Author's collection.*

Jade green cocktail glass, 3", $35. *Author's collection.*

Fry blue cocktail glass with needle-point etch, 4", $35. *Courtesy of Valerie & Bill McCormack.*

Cobalt cocktail glass with crystal stem, 5-1/2", $25. *Author's collection.*

A selection of some of the over fifty items available in Cambridge's "Caprice" line beverage wares: Cambridge #3550 "Caprice" (1936-57) moonlight blue: Back row: #300 water goblet, 9 oz., 7-3/4", $45; #300 wine, 5-3/4", 2.5 oz., $70; #300 ice tea, footed, 12 oz., 6-1/4", $55; #300 water, footed, 10 oz., 5", $45; #179 pitcher, tilt ball, juice jug, 32 oz., 6-3/4", $375; Front row: #310 juice tumbler, flat, 5 oz., 3-3/4", $75; #310 dinner water, flat, 10 oz., 4-1/2", $75; #300 juice, footed, 5 oz., 4", $35; #300 liquor cocktail, 3 oz., 5-1/2", $50. *Courtesy of Roger LeBlanc.*

Crystal cocktail glasses with black stems, 4-1/2", $25 each. *Courtesy of Francois Houle.*

Morgantown #7640 "Art Moderne" crystal stems with ebony (black) stem: 5", $110; cordial, etched monogram "C", 4-1/2", $95. *Courtesy of Francois Houle.*

Crystal with black stem water goblet, floral cut, 7-3/4", $55. *Courtesy of Valerie & Bill McCormack.*

Cambridge "Statuesque" crystal bowl with ebony stem, 6-1/2", $175 each. *Courtesy of Francois Houle.*

Crystal nude stem, believed to be French, 6-3/4", $55. *Courtesy of Valerie & Bill McCormack.*

Heisey #5038 (1942-57) crystal cocktail glass, fancy rooster, designed by Ray Cobel, 5-1/2", $85. *Courtesy of Jeff & Mary Czech.*

Crystal cocktail glass with eagle stem, 6-1/4", $35. *Author's collection.*

Libbey "Kangaroo" crystal cocktail glass, 5-1/4", $95. *Courtesy of Jeff & Mary Czech.*

Crystal cocktail, rooster stem, gold and black, 6", $25. *Author's collection.*

Morgantown #7668 "Galaxy" crystal stems, #787-1/2 "Mayfair" etch: saucer champagne, 5-1/2 oz., $25; cocktail glass, 3-1/2 oz., $20. *Author's collection.*

Duncan Miller "Terrace" crystal saucer champagne, "First Love" etch (c.1937), $35; crystal hollow stem champagne, similar styles made by numerous companies including Cambridge, Heisey, Tiffin, and others, 4", $15. *Author's collection.*

Fostoria #2056 "American" crystal cone-footed cocktail (1935-70), 3 oz., 3-3/4", $12; high foot sherbet (1924-82), 4-1/2 oz., 4-1/2", $10. *Author's collection.*

Heisey #1405 "Ipswich" (1931-46) crystal saucer champagne, 4 oz., 4-1/2", $20; oyster cocktail, 4 oz., 3-1/4", $15. *Author's collection.*

Tiffin crystal with green trim saucer champagne, spiral optic bowl, needle-point etch, 6", $35. *Author's collection.*

Crystal cocktail glass, cut stylized bubbles, 6", $25. *Author's collection.*

Fostoria crystal liquor cocktail glass, #279 "June" etch (1928-52), 5", $20. *Author's collection.*

Libbey/Rock Sharpe #1013 (c.1950) crystal cocktail, "Arvida" cut, 6-1/2", $25; Fostoria #6037 "Silver Flutes" (1949-71) crystal tall sherbet, #343 "Heather" etch, 7 oz., 6", $25. *Author's collection.*

Fenton #1620 "Plymouth" (1933-37) French opalescent high ball tumbler, 8 oz., 4", $25; ice tea tumbler, 12 oz., 6", $30; saucer champagne, 4-1/4", $25; goblet, 5-3/4", $30. *Courtesy of Donna Hatch.*

White opalescent goblet, 5-3/4", $45. *Courtesy of Valerie & Bill McCormack.*

Smoke cocktail glass, clambroth stem, leaf cut, 5-1/4", $25. *Author's collection.*

Duncan Miller #D1 crystal cocktail, "Athena" cut, 4-3/4", $20. *Author's collection.*

Tumblers

Duncan Miller #55 crystal whiskey, "Spider Web" cut, 2", $45. *Courtesy of David C. Cooper.*

Duncan Miller (c. 1940s) crystal shot glass, "Mallard Duck Design" silver intaglio etching, 2-1/4", $25. *Courtesy of David C. Cooper.*

Crystal pousse café (c.1960), footed, cut pattern by J. Morawiec (cutter for Hughes Corn Flower mid-1950s), Toronto, Canada, 4-1/2", $12. *Author's collection.*

Crystal shot glass "What the devil do we care?" (c.1935), sham base, 3-1/2", $20. *Courtesy of Norma Brown.*

Crystal tumbler, "Don't Drink the Water Use Eagle 120 Malt – Eagle Supply House Rochester N.Y.," 3-1/2", $25. *Courtesy of Norma Brown.*

Fenton #1620 "Plymouth" (1933-37) crystal tumblers: high ball, flat, 4", 8 oz., $12; whiskey, flat, 2-1/2 oz., 2-3/4", $15. *Courtesy of Donna Hatch.*

Fenton #35 crystal whiskey (c.1936), "San Toy" acid etched satin, 2-1/2", $12. *Courtesy of Donna Hatch.*

Duncan Miller "Chanticleer" (1920s-30s) frosted crystal old fashioned, 7 oz., 3-1/2", $25; whiskey, 3 oz., 3", $20. *Courtesy of Jeff & Mary Czech.*

"Good Luck" crystal black cat shot glasses, 2-1/4", $8 each. *Author's collection.*

Hocking "Colonial" (1934-36) crystal whiskey, 1-1/2 oz., 2-1/2", $12. *Courtesy of Russ Barker.*.

Silver City "Wolf Head" crystal tumblers, with metal heads, leaf cut, 5-3/4", $125 each.

Crystal old fashioned tumbler, sterling silver overlay "Scottie Dog," 3-1/4", $25. *Author's collection.*

Crystal naughty tumblers, reversible, 4-1/4": gal with sun hat; gal in wedding dress; gal in Victorian attire, $15 each. *Courtesy of Lynda Edwards.*

Reverse peek.

Crystal naughty tumblers, reversible, 4-1/4": milk maid; gal in wedding dress; gal playing croquet, $15 each. *Courtesy of Lynda Edwards.*

Reverse peek.

McKee "Bottoms Up" jadite cocktail tumblers, 3-1/4", $75 each. Black coaster/ash tray, $55. Reproductions have been made. These original tumblers have embossed patent numbers, in this case Pat. 77725, and more detail on the hands. A 1932 ad claimed "new and up-to-the-minute selling appeal. Men and women go for this in a big way. Makes a fast selling bridge prize or gift." Retail price was a dollar for carton of four tumblers. *Courtesy of Valerie & Bill McCormack.*

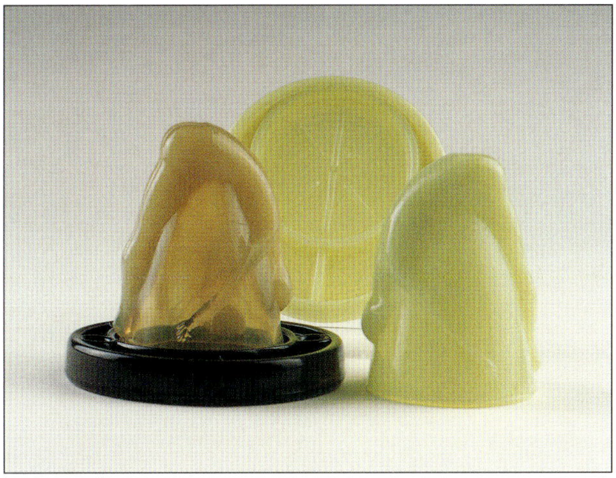

McKee "Bottoms Up" caramel and custard tumblers, 3-1/4", $85 each. Black coaster/ash tray, $55. *Courtesy of Valerie & Bill McCormack.*

McKee "Jolly Golfer" tumblers with hat lid, pink, crystal frosted, green, 5", $65 each.

New Martinsville #37 "Moondrops" (1932-40) green and Ritz blue (cobalt) shot glasses, company's ad declared these to be "reminiscent of the age of chivalry," 2 oz., 2-3/4", $20 each. *Author's collection.*

Crystal tumbler, "Don't Squeeze – Use Fees / Cocktail Mixes / Bitters – Syrups / Fee Brothers since 1863 Rochester N.Y.," 3-1/2", $15. *Courtesy of Donna Hatch.*

Crystal "Bon Voyage" shot glass, when filled to the top "No Survivors," 3-1/4", $15. *Courtesy of Donna Hatch.*

Bartlett-Collins "Scottie Dogs" (c. 1940s) crystal old fashioned tumblers, 3-1/4", $20 each. *Author's collection.*

"Scottie Dogs" (c. 1950s) crystal shot glasses, 2-1/4", $10 each. *Author's collection.*

Green brandy inhalers, crystal foot, 4-1/2", $15 each. *Author's collection.*

Fenton #1700 "Lincoln Inn" (1928-37) high ball tumblers, 12 oz., 5": green $25; ruby $40. *Courtesy of Kathy McCarney.*

West Virginia Specialty ruby shot glass, deco, platinum trim, 2-1/2", $12. Ruby roly poly, 1-3/4", $10. *Author's collection.*

Multicolor tumbler set on metal tray, tumblers, 4-1/2", thought to be European. Set $55. *Author's collection.*

Paden City #191 (1932) Coca Cola tumbler, 12 oz., 5-1/2". "Stolen from McVan's" (McVan's Nite Club, Buffalo New York, "Buffalo's Busiest Bright Spot," c.1947) silk screened on outside, $25. *Courtesy of Valerie & Bill McCormack.*

Pink tumblers, 4-1/4"; tray, with cigarette pack holder, match box holder, and ash tray, 7-1/2" x 6-3/4", set $45. *Courtesy of Valerie & Bill McCormack.*

Beer Mugs & Pilseners

Fostoria milk glass mugs, "Art Decorated" (c.1904), brown fired on monk transfer, miniature, 3-1/4", $45 each. Milk glass mug, 3-1/4", $55. Made on contract for Butler Brothers. *Author's collection.*

Fostoria milk glass mug, "Art Decorated" (c.1904), brown fired on monk transfer, 4-1/2", $55. *Author's collection.*

New Martinsville amber beer mug, 3-1/4", $35. *Author's collection.*

Cambridge #1405 (c.1930) amber beer stein, ground base, one engraved "To B from Marge – Preston 1946," 16 oz., 6", $45 each. *Courtesy of Proctor's Depression Glass.*

"Chesterfield" amber beer mug, 5-1/4", $35. *Courtesy of Valerie & Bill McCormack.*

McKee "Bottoms Up" (1928-33) beer mugs, 5-1/2": custard, $175; jadite, $275. *Courtesy of Valerie & Bill McCormack.*

Imperial #600 "Chesterfield" (c.1930) green beer mug, 5-1/2", $45. Cambridge #550 (c.1930) beer mug, 5-1/2", 10 oz., $45. *Author's collection.*

Fenton green beer mug, 5-1/2", $45; green beer mug, possibly European, 5-1/2", $35. *Courtesy of Proctor's Depression Glass.*

Hocking #636 "Pillar Optic"(1937-42) green beer mug, 4", $45.

Jeannette #516 pink beer mug, ribbed, 16 oz., 5-1/2", $45; pink beer mug, 5-1/2", $55. *Courtesy of Proctor's Depression Glass.*

Seneca #903 "Slim" (c.1932) green pilseners, crystal foot, 8-3/4", $20 each. "Tall and slim, these 16-ounce glasses for long, summer drinks…six different colors – ruby, Florentine green, Royal blue, Ocean blue, burgundy, and amber." *Courtesy of Jeff & Mary Czech.*

Cobalt mugs, made in Japan (c.1945), metal holder with oriental scene and nude handle, 5", $25; 5-1/2", $30. *Author's collection.*

Duncan Miller #54 (c.1934) crystal beer mugs: applied amber handle, 5", $25; applied ruby handle, 3-3/4", $35. "Here's more of that color and dash that you've come to expect in Duncan glassware." The smaller handled mugs were Duncan Miller's failed attempt to set a trend… "Cocktails—and handled, no less!" *Courtesy of Jeff & Mary Czech.*

Indiana crystal saw-tooth beer mug, ruby stained top, 4-3/4", $55. *Author's collection.*

Cambridge "Mt. Vernon" (1931-57) Carmen (ruby) beer mug, crystal handle, 4-1/4", $65. *Courtesy of Proctor's Depression Glass.*

Fenton #1620 "Plymouth" (1933-37) crystal pilsener, 10 oz., 7-1/4", $18. *Courtesy of Donna Hatch.*

Crystal beer mugs: cut floral, 5-1/2", $20; ribbed, 5-1/2", $15. *Author's collection.*

Crystal pilseners (c.1960) decorated, possibly Libbey, 8-1/4", $10 each. *Author's collection.*

Part VI
Bar Accessories

Swizzle Sticks, Muddlers & Coasters

I was in one of my favorite antiquing haunts earlier this year and spotted a strange object—a small round flattened piece of glass with a criss-cross pattern attached to a 4-inch glass rod, in a lovely amethyst shade. The proprietor was perplexed as to the use of such a contraption and had drawn blanks asking many collecting folks. Being somewhat conversant with spirits I blithely informed him that it was a "muddler." Well that didn't turn on any light bulbs! A muddler is one of those necessary bar acoutrements for making the perfect cocktail that involves mint leaves, fruits, or sugars that need to be mashed into a refreshment. Oh yes, one could use the back of a spoon, but these dandy little items are oh so useful besides being delightful mystery items with which to bamboozle the uninitiated.

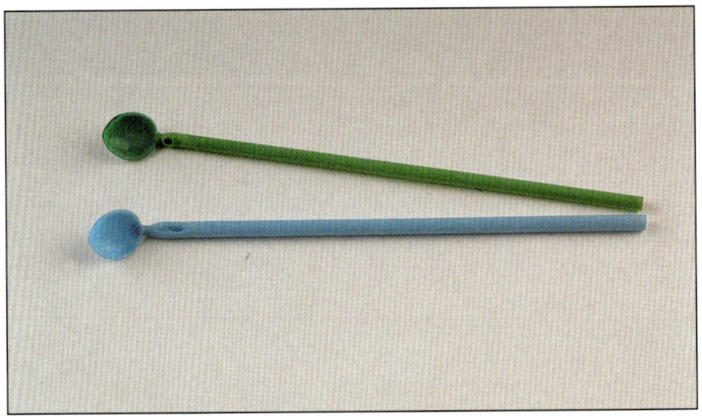

Blue, red, yellow, and green straw-spoons, 8", $15 each. *Courtesy of Donna Hatch.*

Blue, green, yellow, purple, amber swizzle sticks, novelty liquid filled, 7", $12 each. *Courtesy of Valerie & Bill McCormack.*

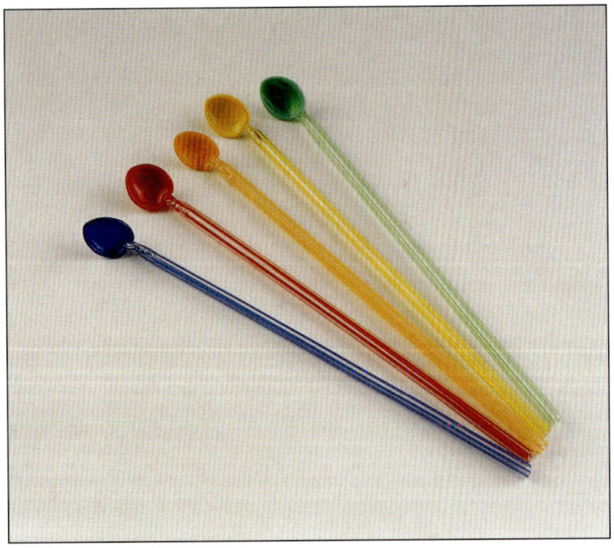

Jadite and delphite straw-spoons, 8-1/4", $20 each. *Courtesy of Valerie & Bill McCormack.*

Blue, purple, and green muddler-swizzle sticks, 5-1/2", $10 each. *Courtesy of Valerie & Bill McCormack.*

Morgantown "Filament" crystal muddlers, cased colored filaments, ball end, 5": Stiegel Green $55; Golden Iris (amberina) $65; Spanish Red $65; Ritz Blue $75. Introduced by Morgantown in 1935 and sold for $1.75 to $2.00 for a card of six muddlers. *Courtesy of Jeff & Mary Czech.*

Cambridge #1 green muddler, 4-1/2", $25. *Courtesy of Jeff & Mary Czech.*

Amber, blue, red, and green muddlers, 4", $7 each. *Courtesy of Valerie & Bill McCormack.*

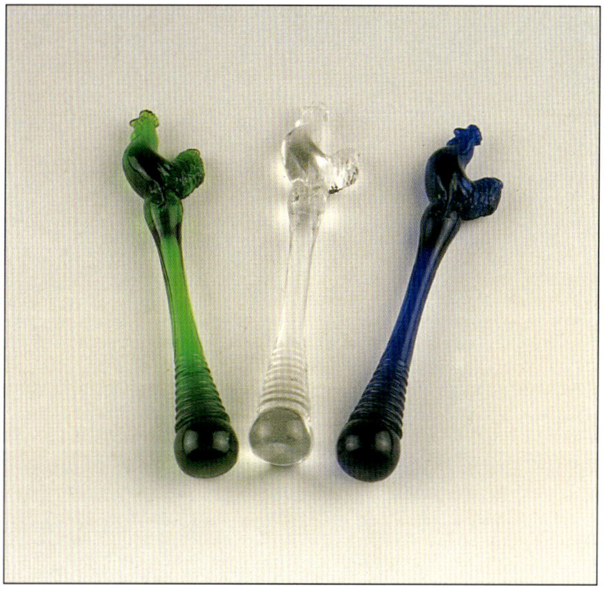

Cambridge #2 "Rooster" muddlers, 5-1/2": forest green, $250; crystal, $25; cobalt, $225.

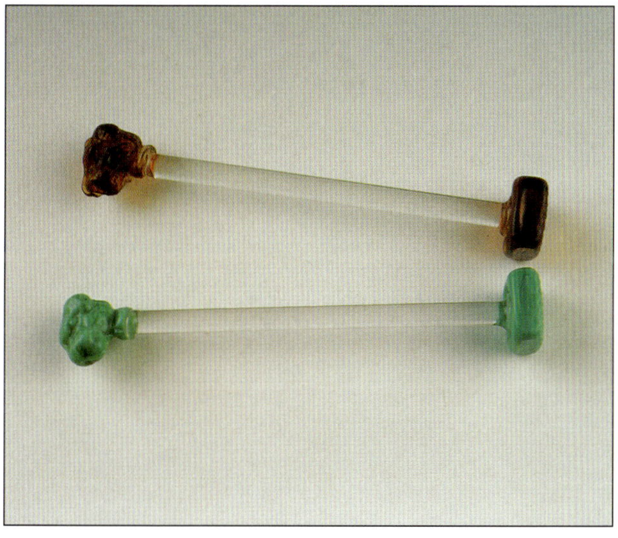

"Dog Head" figural green and brown muddlers, crystal stems, 5", $20 each. *Courtesy of Valerie & Bill McCormack.*

Swizzle sticks, green, crystal, yellow, amber, with caricature heads, 11", each, $20. *Courtesy of Valerie & Bill McCormack.*

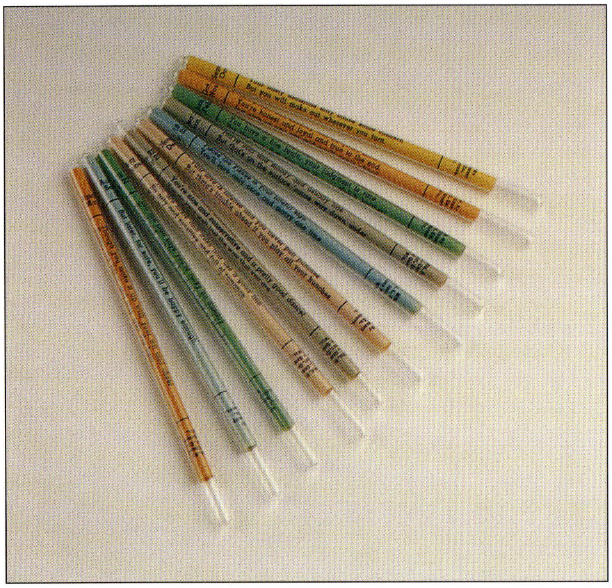

Crystal "Horoscope" multicolor swizzle sticks, color paper inserts, 6", $5 each. A new fortune for each month. J. L. Chaney Inst. Co. Taurus – April/May "You are a bull called Taurus the horrible. Your furious temper is sometimes deplorable, though you make it up with your wit and cheer. Forget the liquor and stay with the beer."

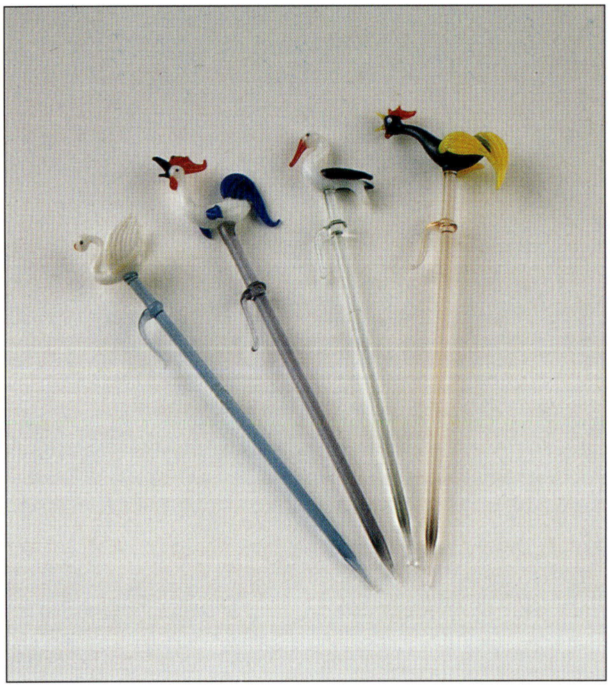

Czechoslovakian multicolor bird figural cocktail picks, 4-1/2", $10 each. Note the hook on the side for hanging these. *Courtesy of Valerie & Bill McCormack.*

Crystal swizzle stick, paper insert advertising Bellow's whiskey, Bellow's & Co., NY, 6", $8.

Czechoslovakian multicolor rooster cocktail picks, 3-3/4", $10 each. *Courtesy of Donna Hatch.*

Imperial #400/19 "Candlewick" crystal muddler, $25. *Author's collection.*

Crystal swizzle sticks advertising mini 45 records: green label RCA Victor, "The Touch of God's Hands," from "When It's Roundup Time in Heaven" by Eddy Arnold (1954); black label Decca, "No One But You" by the Mills Brothers, 5-1/2", $20 each. *Courtesy of Valerie & Bill McCormack.*

The flip side: RCA Victor: "The Chapel on the Hill"; Decca: "An Ri Rung."

Fostoria #2510 "Sunray" (1935-44) crystal coaster, 4-1/4", $8. Fostoria #2056 "American" (1915-87) crystal coaster, 3-1/2", $10. *Courtesy of Suzanne Fry.*

Heisey #1540 "Lariat" (1941-57) crystal coaster, 4", $10; Heisey #1503 "Crystolite" (1937-57) crystal coaster, 4", $10; Heisey "Ridgleigh" crystal coaster or cocktail rest, 3-3/4", $15. *Courtesy of Suzanne Fry.*

Imperial #160/1R "Cape Cod" (1932-84) crystal coaster-ash tray, 4-1/2", $10; Anchor Hocking #700/702 "Early American Prescut" crystal coaster, 3-3/4", $4. *Courtesy of Suzanne Fry.*

Heisey #1469 "Ridgleigh" (1935-44) crystal coaster or cocktail rest, 3-3/4", $15; Hocking "Queen Mary" (1936-49) crystal coaster, 3-1/2", $4; Hocking "Manhattan" (1938-43) crystal coaster, 3-1/2", $15. *Courtesy of Suzanne Fry.*

Jeannette "Cherry Blossom" (1930-39) green coaster, 3-1/4", $12; Jeannette "Adam" (1932-34) green coaster, 3-3/4", $20; Hazel Atlas "Florentine No. 2" or "Poppy No. 2" (1932-35) green coaster, 3-1/4", $12. *Courtesy of Suzanne Fry.*

Jeannette "Windsor Diamond" (1936-46) green coaster, 3-1/4", $18; green coaster, rayed, 3-1/4", $8; Jeannette "Cubist" (1929-33) green coaster, 3-1/4", $10. *Courtesy of Suzanne Fry.*

MacBeth-Evans #7685 pink coaster, spiral, 3-1/4", $10; green coaster, spiral, patent no. 1662146 filed by G. C. Elliott on April 7, 1927, 4-1/4", $12. *Courtesy of Suzanne Fry.*

Jeannette "Cherry Blossom" (1930-39) pink coaster, 3-1/4", $12; Jeannette "Floral" (1931-35) pink coaster, 3-1/4", $12. *Courtesy of Suzanne Fry.*

Hocking #2500 "Miss America" (1935-38) pink coaster, same as the sherbet plate but with ribs (I found a coaster in my pile of sherbet plates after this photo shoot. Sherbet plates sell for around $10 each. A very pleasant find!), 5-1/2", $35; Jeannette "Homespun" or "Fine Rib" (1939-49) pink coaster-ash tray, 3-3/4", $7. *Courtesy of Suzanne Fry.*

Hazel-Atlas "Rayed Center" coasters, 3-3/4": green $10; Ritz blue $12; pink $10. *Courtesy of Valerie & Bill McCormack.*

Cambridge #3550 "Caprice" (1936-57) Moonlight blue coaster, 3-1/2", $25. *Courtesy of Suzanne Fry.*

Jade coasters, 3", in covered box, 3-1/2" x 3", set $55. Custard coasters only, set of 4, $25. *Courtesy of Valerie & Bill McCormack.*

Bitters Bottles, Snack Jars, Etcetera

Something about bitters bottles appeals to me; then again—thinking about it—most everything involving barware appeals to me. These smallish bottles, usually topped with a metal tube device held in with a cork collar, are used for doling out minute portions, several drops at a time, of particular alcoholic ingredients for one's cocktail. Attempting to ascertain the makers of these little objects is somewhat tricky—not too much effort was evidently put into designing them, so many do look quite similar.

Vintage snack jars are few and far between. To an aficionado of a cool pint, like myself, they are a necessity. The British influence certainly shows through in the "Crisps" jar pictured below, while the Hocking pretzel jars are much more American in spirit. Hocking Glass Company's "8-piece Beer & Pretzel Set" (see page 129) is right up my line!

Frosted crystal bitters bottle, green and white decoration, 5-3/4", $25. *Courtesy of Valerie & Bill McCormack.*

Crystal bitters bottle, zipper pattern, white lettering, 8", $30. *Author's collection.*

Crystal bitters bottle, 5-1/2", $30. *Courtesy of Jeff & Mary Czech.*

Crystal bitters bottle, cut lettering, 7", $35. *Courtesy of David C. Cooper.*

Crystal whiskey flask, leather covered, 5-1/2", $35. *Author's collection.*

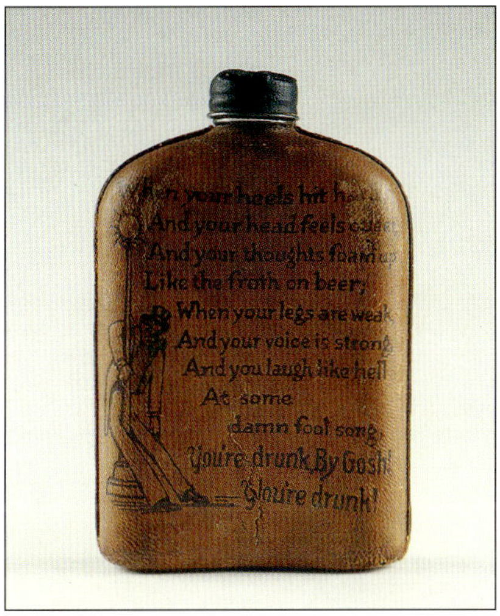

Reverse of whiskey flask.

Crystal whiskey flask, spiral optic, 5-1/2", $25. *Author's collection.*

Scottie Dog tray, glass/wood/metal, 13-1/4" x 7", $35. *Author's collection.*

Fenton "Elephant Whiskey" crystal bottle, embossed "Federal Law forbids sale or reuse of this bottle R-344-9855," 8", $95. *Courtesy of Donna Hatch.*

"Chelton House Rock Candy in Rock 'n Rye Jar," 7", 6 oz., $35. "To make Rock and Rye add one slice Orange, one slice Lemon and enough Whiskey to cover Rock Candy. Allow to stand overnight. After about 1/3 of jar is consumed refill with Whiskey. Rock Candy makes any Whiskey smoother and more mellow and is a very satisfying drink in itself. A Wonderful Cough Mixture..." *Author's collection.*

Huether's jadite shaker (c.1935), advertising a different beer on each face: "Try Huether's Wuerzberger Beer, Pilsener Beer, Half and Half, Olde Tyme Stock Ale." $250. The Huether Hotel is still in operation in Kitchener, Ontario, Canada and happily enough is still serving up three of these fine refreshments, plus many others. Their pilsener is now called Lion Lager. Brew master and historian Kelly Adlys' family has run the business for the past fifty years.

Reverse view.

Fostoria #2056 "American" (1915-86) crystal straw holder, cover missing, 8", $275. *Courtesy of Valerie & Bill McCormack.*

Crystal straw holder, brass and steel lid, No. 1276338, Aug 20, 1918, 12-1/2", $125. *Courtesy of Valerie & Bill McCormack.*

Crystal straw holder, metal lid, 11-1/2", $100. *Courtesy of Francois Houle.*

Fenton #1620 "Plymouth" (1933-37) crystal jigger, 1 side, 1 oz., other side, 2 oz., 4-1/4", $45. *Courtesy of Donna Hatch.*

Crystal "Smith's Potato Crisps" jar, deco plastic lid, 9", $125. *Courtesy of Valerie & Bill McCormack.*

Hocking #695 "Pillar Optic" (1937-42) green pretzel jar, 130 oz., 10-1/2", $155. Also came in pink, crystal, and frosted crystal. Crystal was also decorated with multicolor stripes. *Author's collection.*

Hocking "Rings" (c.1935) crystal ice chopper, 10", $35. *Courtesy of Russ Barker.*

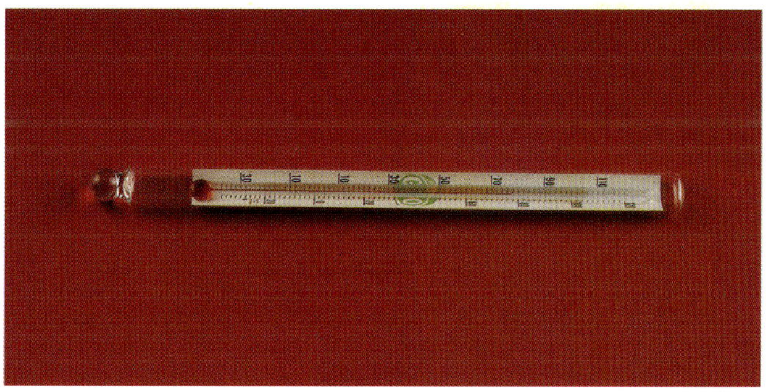

Crystal beverage thermometer, "stir until drink reaches proper temperature indicated by green spot—then GO!", Pat. No. 2246241 Made in USA, 6-1/4", $25. *Courtesy of Norma Brown.*

Juice Reamers

Towards the back of the 1941 book, *Here's How – Mixed Drinks* with its novel leather and metal-hinged wooden cover, author W.C. Whitfield adds some "Points to Remember." Point number seven is: "Lemon or orange juice will not keep perfectly fresh, even in a modern refrigerator. For best results, squeeze your juices as you need them." The ideal item with which to accomplish this is the glass juice reamer. Reamers come in three sizes—the smaller one is for lemons and limes, the medium-sized one takes care of oranges, while the more elusive largest size is for grapefruits. These are generally handled for ease in pouring the juice into mixers or pitchers. A bit harder to come by are the pitchers that are topped off with a reamer. These well-designed reamers were made with holes in the base to allow the fresh juice to flow into the jug. Scarcer yet are the cocktail shakers with combination metal cocktail lid and reamer top. Paden City Glass made the majority of these nifty combo items. While many of the commoner reamers may be found for between $15 and $35, since the opportunity arose I have pictured mainly highly sought after, scarcer reamers with considerably dearer prices.

McKee "Saunders" reamers, "Witch's Hat," 6": black $1650; jadite $1500. *Courtesy of Valerie & Bill McCormack.*

McKee "Sunkist" orange reamers, 6": Front row: chocolate $750; opalescent white $125; Crown Tuscan $375; Back row: black $750; Seville (yellow) $55; jadite $55. *Courtesy of Valerie & Bill McCormack.*

McKee "Sunkist" grapefruit reamers, embossed, 6" x 8": Jadite $255; Chalaine (blue), $750; Seville (yellow) $225. *Courtesy of Valerie & Bill McCormack.*

Jeannette 2-cup measure with #245 reamer, sunflower embossed base: jadite $85; delphite $175. *Courtesy of Valerie & Bill McCormack.*

"Fleur-de-Lis" red-orange reamer, 6", $350. *Courtesy of Valerie & Bill McCormack.*

Fenton #1619 (1933) jade green 2-piece reamer and handled jug set, 5", $1000. *Courtesy of Valerie & Bill McCormack.*

Fry "Blue Goose" pearl opalescent white reamer, embossed "Blue Goose," 6", $450. "Blue Goose" sign, "Distributed by American Fruit Growers Inc. Los Angeles California," 11-1/2" x 11-1/4", $45. *Courtesy of Valerie & Bill McCormack.*

Hazel-Atlas "Criss Cross," left to right: pink lemon reamer, 5", $275; pink orange reamer, 6", $250; green orange reamer, 6", $30; cobalt orange reamer, 6", $300; green lemon reamer, 5", $35. *Courtesy of Valerie & Bill McCormack.*

Hazel-Atlas 2-cup measure and reamer set, 5-1/2": yellow $350; green $75; pink $125. *Courtesy of Valerie & Bill McCormack.*

U.S. Glass green reamer-pitcher, with lid, 11", $275. *Courtesy of Valerie & Bill McCormack.*

U.S. Glass measuring cup-reamer, embossed snowflake on base, 8", $95. *Courtesy of Valerie & Bill McCormack.*

Paden City #191 "Party Line" combination cocktail shaker-reamer, 10": amber with gold encrusted band, $55; pink with floral cut, $75; green $75. *Courtesy of Valerie & Bill McCormack.*

Medicinal & Morning After

A pioneering crusader who helped form the Temperance movement in the 1800s was Reverend Theobald Mathew (1790-1856). The Reverend's pledge was circulated for signatures in hopes of raising awareness: "I promise to abstain from all intoxicating drinks except used medicinally and by order of a medical man; and to discountenance the cause and practice of intemperance." The movement tottered along for decades, put off track by the Civil War. By the 1890s, Anti-Saloon Leagues became increasingly active politically, running slates of candidates who supported their cause and pressuring legislators to draft laws against alcohol production. World War One was the pivotal point in this struggle for a "dry" lifestyle, as abstention was felt to be a patriotic duty by many during wartime. The National Prohibition Act, the 18th Amendment to the United States Constitution, was instituted on 16 January, 1920. Manufacturing, selling, transporting, importing or exporting of intoxicating liquor was prohibited.

One of the major players in the production of whisky as medicine was the Walter B. Duffy Distilling Company of Rochester, New York. In 1886, they began making their Duffy's Pure Malt Whisky. They were to be at the center of legal wranglings concerning food purity a mere fifteen years later.

Harvey W. Wiley, M.D. of the U.S. Bureau of Chemistry (forerunner of the FDA, the Food and Drug Administration) was deeply involved in the legal battles over food purity. The question "What is whisky?" was fiercely fought over the first decade of the twentieth century. Wiley wrote, "Whisky is used extensively as a medicine. Physicians differ widely in regard to its medicinal value. The greater number of physicians think it has medicinal value. A very respectable number look upon whisky as unsuitable for any medicinal purpose whatever." During the terrible influenza epidemic of 1918-1919, many physicians argued that spirits saved many lives. The 1924 U.S. Senate hearings on Prohibition heard from physicians who recommended malt liquors for "convalescence, improving the appetite, neurasthenia, senile decay, malnutrition, lowered vitality, digestive ailments, wasting diseases and nursing mothers." After Prohibition, the number of prescriptions filled by some doctors skyrocketed. Suspicious minds might start to think that not all these were above-board and for purely medicinal purposes. Indeed, one instance of issuing a "forty-ounce prescription for an allegedly ill cow" was perhaps taking things a tad too far!

The rub was that by the introduction of a Pure Food Law, products such as Duffy's Malt Whiskey and Canadian Club Whiskey, which were blended or distilled from anything other than grain, would have to be called "imitation whiskey." The lobbying was fierce to get this damaging wording changed. It was in the best interests of Duffy's to have it declared that "whisky as a drug was a different product from whisky as a beverage." A 1916 report from the New Haven Department of Health noted that Duffy's Malt Whiskey was "A slightly sweetened whiskey made from rectified spirit. Alcohol about 450%. Therapeutic claims greatly exaggerated." As Cheryl Kresniak Warsh so succinctly stated in *Drink in Canada: historical essays*, "Alcohol was both medicine and poison, creative and destructive."

Cobalt "Bromo Seltzer" (c.1930) dispenser and tumbler, cobalt base, metal stem, 15-1/2", $255. Original label read "Bromo Seltzer Fast Relief for Simple Headache, Upset Stomach…" *Courtesy of Valerie & Bill McCormack.*

Green coffee dispenser, ribbed, metal base and stem, Bakelite lid, 15-1/2", $355. *Courtesy of Valerie & Bill McCormack.*

"Duffy's Pure Malt Whiskey" crystal measure cup, handled, "A Medicine," measurements for "Table, Dessert, Tea", 3-3/4" x 1-3/4", $55. *Courtesy of Vi Brennan.*

"Duffy's Pure Malt Whiskey" crystal measure cup, top view.

Part VII
Barware Sets

Starting in the mid-20s, many of the items produced for the bar were parts of larger sets, providing the perfect host and hostess a full range of items with which to fulfill all entertaining requirements—plates, bowls, tumblers, pitchers, platters, serving bowls, ash trays, relishes, etcetera. With the end of Prohibition in 1933, sets of glassware specially designed with bar use in mind came onto the the market in a vast avalanche of choices.

Duncan Miller #503 "Touraine" crystal martini glass, Laurel Wreath cut, 4-1/4", $25 each; #11 cocktail shaker, 10", $110; #529 crystal decanter, 10-1/4", $95. *Courtesy of David C. Cooper.*

Duncan Miller crystal with "Mallard Ducks" etch: old fashioned tumbler, 3-1/4", $25 each; cocktail shaker, 11", $125; #115 "Canterbury" (1938-55) handled martini pitcher, 9-1/4", $95. *Courtesy of David C. Cooper.*

Duncan Miller "Terrace" (1935-55) crystal cocktail glasses, "First Love" etch, 3-3/4", $45 each; #500 crystal cocktail shaker, 11-1/4", $300; #115 "Canterbury" (1938-55) crystal pitcher and stir stick, 80 oz., 9-1/4", $255. *Courtesy of David C. Cooper.*

MacBeth-Evans crystal with frosted crystal and platinum trim: cocktail glass, footed, 3-1/2", $12; cocktail shaker, 11", $55; high ball tumbler, 5", $10; handled martini pitcher, 10", $45; tumbler, 3-1/4", $6. *Courtesy of David C. Cooper.*

Hocking "Cameo" (1930-34) crystal decanter with stopper, 10", $275; cocktail shaker (rare), 11-1/4", $1200.

Bartlett-Collins crystal barware items with #806 "Golden Grape" decoration (c.1942): goblet, 16 oz., 6-1/4", $15; ice tub, 4-1/4", $25; #1105 tumbler, 5 oz., $8; #1109-1/2 tumbler, 9-1/2 oz., 4-3/4", $12; #28 jug, 32 oz., 6-1/4", $25. *Courtesy of Lynda Edwards.*

Hocking "Cameo" (1930-34) green decanter with stopper, 10", $225; ice tub, 3", $200.

Hocking G600/12 "Pillar Optic" (c. 1932) "8-piece Beer and Pretzel Set" consisting of one G695 green pretzel jar and cover, 130 oz., 10-1/2", $155; one G680 green jug, 80 oz., 8-1/4", $45; six G636 beer mugs, 12 oz., 4", $35 each.

Imperial #600 "Chesterfield" beer set: green mugs, 5-1/2", $45 each; beer pitcher, 8-1/4", $95. *Courtesy of Jeff & Mary Czech.*

McKee jade pinch decanter, 9-1/2", $355; Seville (yellow) "Bottom's Up" mug, 5-1/2", $175; jade pinch water bottle, 5", $225; jade "Bottom's Up" mug, 5-1/2", $275; Seville pinch decanter, 9-1/2", $225. *Courtesy of Valerie & Bill McCormack.*

Fenton #1620 "Plymouth" (1933-37) ruby: sherbet, 6 oz., 4", $20; wine, 4 oz., 4", $20; cocktail shaker, 32 oz., $225; old fashioned tumbler, 3-1/2", 7 oz., $25. *Courtesy of Donna Hatch.*

Cobalt cocktail glass, ribbed, metal base, deco, 4-1/2", $15 each; "Prime Rib" bowl with metal base, 4-1/2" x 9", $55; "Standing Rib" cocktail shaker, 10-3/4", $95. *Courtesy of Valerie & Bill McCormack.*

Imperial #711 "Big Shots" (c.1955) green "Magnum" cocktail mixer, came originally with a wooden "Shot-gun Cleaning Rod" stirrer, 40 oz., $85; "Little Shot" whiskey, 2-1/2 oz., $15; "Half Shot" cocktail, 5 oz., $12, "Sure Shot" tumbler, 11 oz., $15, "Big Shot" highball, 14 oz., $20. The set was designed to match Winchester ammunition. *Courtesy of David C. Cooper.*

Part VIII
Corn Flower Cut Barware

Corn Flower-cut glass made by the W. J. Hughes Corn Flower Company (1916-1988) remains one of the hottest of collectibles on the Canadian antique market. Although there are numerous variations of cornflowers cut on glassware, the Hughes Corn Flower cut features a 12-petalled flower, grid-like interior, and elegant sweeping stems. As with other barware in this volume, most of the colored Corn Flower dates from the mid-1920s through the mid-1940s. This is the most sought after of all Hughes glassware. Perhaps scarcer even than the colored wares, and equally pricey, are items decorated with gold edging. The Candlewick 400/20 punch bowl set is a showy favorite with advanced collectors. I suspect that there may only have been three dozen ever made—the number from the massive 1953 order of Imperial Candlewick (a boxcar full of some 155,000 items!). With the Corn Flower cut, the 15-piece punch bowl set will fetch three to four times the price of an uncut set. One of my personal favorite items is Imperial's #100 boot-shaped toothpick holder-whiskey tumbler. A shot from that tumbler will give you a double kick! Please refer to my *Elegant Glass with Corn Flower* for additional Corn Flower cut barware.

Polish beer mugs with ruby applied handles, 4", $95 each.
Courtesy of Brenda Beckett.

Federal crystal beer glass, 5-1/4", $20.
Courtesy of Brenda Beckett.

West Virginia Glass Specialty crystal brandy snifter, 4-3/4", $25. Hughes also ordered brandy snifters from Federal Glass and Ferunion (Hungary) in sizes ranging from 4 to 120 ounces.
Courtesy of Brenda Beckett.

Imperial #100 (c.1940) crystal "Boot" shot glasses, left hand had 10-petal flower, right with bud cut, 2-1/2", $45 each. *Courtesy of Brenda Beckett.*

Federal crystal old fashioned tumbler, 3-1/2", $12; Paden City #2003 or Imperial #400/142 "Candlewick" (1937-43) tumbler, sham base, 3-1/4", $20. Both Paden City and Imperial decorated what appear to be identical tumblers during the same era. Hughes bought glass from both firms. With the preponderance of Imperial cuts and colors found on this shape we lean towards Imperial as the maker and supplier to both Paden City and Hughes Corn Flower. *Author's collection.*

Tiffin #020 (c.1935) crystal cocktail, 4-1/2, $25; cordial, 4-1/4, $25; saucer champagne, 4-1/2, $25; water goblet, 6-1/2, $30. *Courtesy of Brenda Beckett.*

Tiffin #020 (c.1935) crystal, gold trim: water goblet, 6-1/2", $85; tumbler, 3-3/4", $55; saucer champagne, 4", $75; liner plate, 5", $45. *Courtesy of Brenda Beckett.*

Ferunion (c.1967) crystal decanter with stopper, 30 oz., 9-1/2", $75. Starting in the mid-1960s, W. J. Hughes Corn Flower began out-sourcing glass cutting overseas. The Corn Flowers cut by the Hungarian firm Ferunion for Hughes tend to have larger interior cross-hatched portions, making the flower appear rounder. *Courtesy of Brenda Beckett.*

Imperial #625 (c.1960) crystal decanter with stopper, 30 oz., 10-1/4", $95. *Courtesy of Brenda Beckett.*

Crystal cigarette box with lid, ribbed, 4-1/2" x 3-1/2", $95. *Courtesy of Brenda Beckett.*

Crystal round ash trays, 5", $12 each. *Courtesy of Brenda Beckett.*

Viking #1150 "Epic" (c.1960) ash tray, 15-1/2", $45. *Courtesy of Brenda Beckett.*

Paden City #191 "Party Line" crystal cordial, 3-1/2", $20 each; ice tub, tab handles, 6", $125. *Courtesy of Brenda Beckett.*

Duncan Miller #28 crystal ice bucket (scarce), 6", $350. *Courtesy of Patrick Doherty.*

Imperial #400/20 "Candlewick" crystal punch set, 6-quart bowl, 17" plate, 12 cups, ladle, $575. Note that the Corn Flower cut punch set sells for three to four times the price of an uncut set. There may have only been thirty-six of these ever cut, those ordered in the 1953 boxcar-load shipment of some 155,000 pieces of Candlewick to W. J. Hughes Corn Flower. *Courtesy DCMA.*

Imperial #400/134 crystal cigarette box with domed cover, 5-1/4", $75. *Courtesy of Lynda Edwards.*

U.S. Glass #8404 pink decanter, 9-1/2", $275; wine, 2-3/4", $65. *Courtesy of Brenda Beckett.*

New Martinsville #37 "Moondrops" green tumbler, 3-1/2", $75; green mug, 6-3/4", $255. Also found in amber and crystal. *Courtesy DCMA.*

Tiffin #196 yellow water goblet, 6-1/2", $85; saucer champagne, 4-1/2", $75; oyster cocktail, 3-3/4", $75; sundae, 3-1/2",$55. *Courtesy DCMA.*

Duncan Miller #28 amber ice bucket, 6", $425. *Courtesy DCMA.*

Part IX

Smoking Items

Cigarette Boxes

A cocktail in one hand and a cigarette in the other was for quite some time the height of sophistication. One only has to look to the silver screen to see the elegant and debonair poses of so many famous starlettes and leading men from yesteryear. Helpful books and pamphlets from the 1930s through the '60s show that proper table settings wouldn't be quite complete without individual ash trays and a box or jar of cigarettes at hand.

Cigarette boxes come in many varieties. Some are flat to the table, some are footed, and some, like the fabulous Cambridge "Statuesque" cigarette box, have a stemmed foot. A number of these could even serve dual purpose as a cigarette box or a box for playing cards.

Greensburg #2 black elephant finial cigarette box, 2-3/4", $75. *Courtesy of Francois Houle.*

Heisey #1489-1/2 "Horse Head" crystal cigarette box, designed by Thomas Clarence Heisey, 4"x 4", $75. Also available in a larger 6-1/4"x 4" size, $125. *Courtesy of Francois Houle.*

Crystal 3-part cigarette box, metal feet and lid, 3-1/2" x 6-1/2", $35. *Author's collection.*

Jeannette #3400/4/P "Butterfly" (c.1958) crystal cigarette box, gold trim, 6-1/4" x 4", $55; matching ash tray, 4", $12. *Courtesy of Tracy Wills.*

Jeannette #207 (c.1934) green cigarette jar, brass embossed lid, 3-3/4", $25. *Author's collection.*

New Martinsville crystal cigarette box, with jade lid, 3-3/4" x 2-3/4", $45. *Author's collection.*

Fostoria "Baroque" Topaz (yellow) cigarette box, with ash tray holder, 3-1/2" x 5-1/2", $75. *Author's collection.*

Westmoreland #555 "English Hobnail" (1917-1940s) green cigarette box, 4-1/2" x 2-1/2", $35; ash tray, 4-1/2", $25. *Courtesy of Jennie Bergman.*

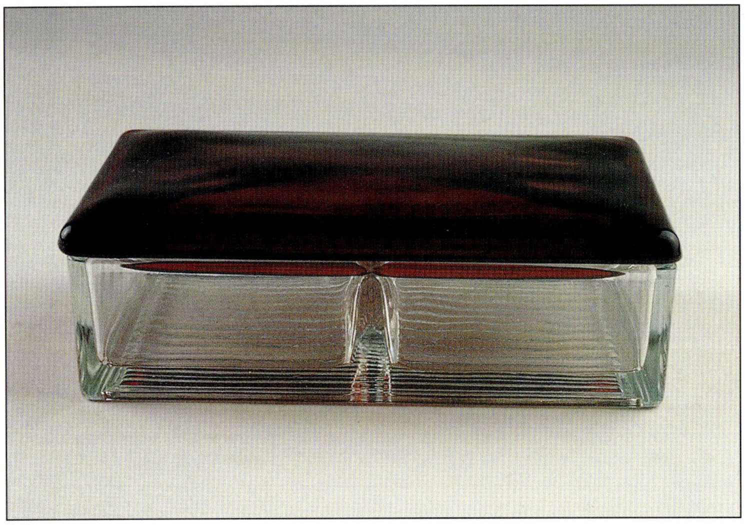

Hocking "Royal Ruby" 2-part crystal cigarette box, ruby lid, 4" x 6", $35. *Courtesy of Valerie & Bill McCormack.*

Cambridge #3011 "Figure Stem Line," "Statuesque" (c.1930) Carmen (ruby) cigarette box and lid, crystal stem, $450.

Akro Agate #803 "Mexicali" marbleized white and green cigarette jar and lid, 4-1/2", $45. Made for Pickwick Cosmetic Corp., New York. "Men's Shaving Soap and Cigarette Jar, Mexican Spice Scent Bath Powder Cigarette Jar, Contents removable: Jar becomes ideal container for cigarettes." *Courtesy of Kathy McCarney.*

Greensburg black table lamp with cigarette box and ash tray, #1 crystal terrier lid, 9-1/2", chrome shade, $95. *Courtesy of Jeff & Mary Czech.*

Cigarette Holders

Neatly designed cigarette holders are so very elegant. Although not seen in use for holding cigarettes any longer (they are too small for the larger cigarettes of the present day), many folks love to use these for business card holders. They are an ideal size for this purpose—and of course look great!

Amber cigarette holder, embossed roses, 3-3/4", $55. *Author's collection.*

Black cigarette holder, 4-1/2", $35. *Author's collection.*

New Martinsville #2003 blue cigarette holder, hand-painted deco ship, 4-1/4", $75. *Author's collection.*

Westmoreland #352 blue cigarette holder, round, 4", $45. *Courtesy of Proctor's Depression Glass.*

Cobalt blue umbrella cigarette holder-ash tray, brass ash tray base, 7", $75. *Courtesy of Valerie & Bill McCormack.*

Fry crystal cigarette holder with green foot, round, 4-1/4", $55. *Courtesy of Valerie & Bill McCormack.*

Fostoria #2354 (1927) green cigarette holder with bulldog etch, 4-1/2", $95; green with floral cut, 5-3/4", $55. *Courtesy of Proctor's Depression Glass.*

Diamond #900 "Adam's Rib" (c.1925) green cigarette holder, ribbed, 4-1/4", $35. *Author's collection.*

Fostoria #5092 crystal cigarette holder, green foot, round, 4-1/2", $55. *Courtesy of Jeff & Mary Czech.*

Fry Emerald Golden Glow (green) cigarette holder (c.1925), crystal base, 4-1/4", $55. *Courtesy of Valerie & Bill McCormack.*

Cambridge #1066 "Aurora" (c.1930) Forest green cigarette holder, crystal base, 5", $65. *Courtesy of Jeff & Mary Czech.*

Lighters

Glass cigarette and cigar lighters from the 1920s and '30s often came with a combination holder and ash tray. Most often found are the slag glass lighters made by the L. J. Houze Convex Glass Company (1914-present) of Point Marion, Pennsylvania. Some fine research has been done lately to help illuminate the production of this firm (and to distinguish it from the Vidrio Glass Company...the question remains, "Did Houze produce all the Vidrio Glass products?"). More information exists and hopefully will soon be released for many anxious students of vintage glass.

Houze (c.1931) yellow/custard with brown and tan veined electric lighter, squat round, 3-footed, 2", $35. *Courtesy of Valerie & Bill McCormack.*

Houze (c.1931) yellow/custard with brown veining dog figural electric lighter, 4-1/4", $45. The Houze trade name for this marbleized glass was On-X-Glass. The white metal figurals were made for Houze by Almar Metal Arts. *Courtesy of Valerie & Bill McCormack.*

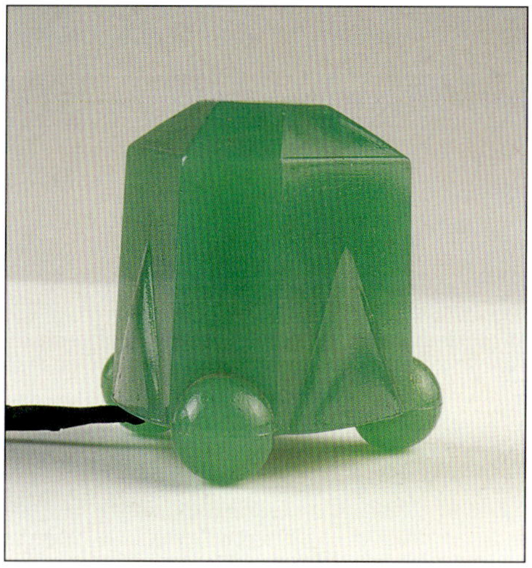

Vidrio "The Royal" (c.1932) jadite electric lighter, deco triangular, ball-shaped 3 feet, 3-3/4", $65. *Courtesy of Valerie & Bill McCormack.*

Jadite deco electric lighter, paneled, 3-footed, 2-1/4", $45. *Courtesy of Valerie & Bill McCormack.*

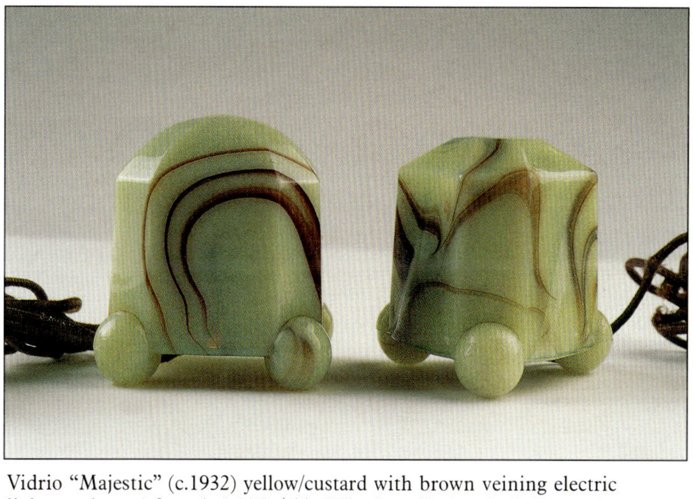

Vidrio "Majestic" (c.1932) yellow/custard with brown veining electric lighters, deco, 4-footed, 3-3/4", $55; "The Royal" electric lighter, 3-footed, $55. *Courtesy of Valerie & Bill McCormack.*

Vidrio "Globe" (c.1932) yellow/custard with brown veining electric lighter, round, 3-footed, 3", $65. *Courtesy of Valerie & Bill McCormack.*

Delphite blue electric lighter, deco tiered, 4-1/4", $65. *Courtesy of Valerie & Bill McCormack.*

Fenton (late 1960s) yellow, ruby, and amberina free-form or swirl lighters, $35 each. *Courtesy of Donna Hatch.*

Vidrio (c.1932) blue marbleized combination electric cigar and cigarette lighter and ash tray. Lighter 2-1/2"; tray 3-3/4" x 2", $75. *Courtesy of Valerie & Bill McCormack.*

Vidrio (c.1932) orange marbleized combination electric cigar and cigarette lighter and ash tray. Lighter 2-1/2"; tray 3-3/4" x 2", $55. *Courtesy of Valerie & Bill McCormack.*

Ash Trays

If you think of an ash tray as nothing more than a round slab of glass with a couple of indentations at the edges, then you haven't looked at the marvels of ingenuity that so many designers over the years have conjured up. From swans to top hats, boats to hearts, playing cards to ducks, the range of shapes is astounding.

Jeannette "Sunflower" (c.1935) green ash tray, 3-3/4", $25; Hazel-Atlas "Checkerboard" green ash tray, 4", $12. *Author's collection.*

Green ash tray , match box holder, embossed "Harrison Hotel Chicago," 4", $35. *Courtesy of Valerie & Bill McCormack.*

U.S. Glass green coaster-ash tray, fan-shape, marked U.S. Glass patented, sold as the "New U.S. Bridge Set." Also sold along with "Primo" pattern tumblers although the coaster does not have the pattern, 4-3/4", $15; green figure eight ash tray, 3-3/4", $15. *Courtesy of Tracy Wills.*

Hazel-Atlas #757-1/2 (c.1936) green ash tray, with attached toilet receptacle complete with hinged seat and lid, 4", $25. *Courtesy of Pat Kurtz.*

Green ash tray, deco, 4-1/4", $15; Jeannette #253 (c.1934) green ash tray, 3-3/4", $15. *Courtesy of Tracy Wills.*

Heisey #357 "Duck" (1928-33) Moongleam (green) ash tray, marked with diamond H, 2-3/4", $155. *Courtesy of Jeff & Mary Czech.*

Green pipe rest ash tray with match box holder, hand painted, 6" diameter, $55. *Courtesy of Valerie & Bill McCormack.*

Green deco ash tray, 2-1/4", $25. *Courtesy of Tracy Wills.*

Cambridge #3400 (1940s) Peach-blo (pink) ash receiver, 2-3/4", $45. *Courtesy of Tracy Wills.*

MacBeth-Evans (c.1932) pink ash tray, marked "MacBeth-Evans Charleroi PA" with figure of a glass blower, 3-1/4", $20; #7541-A pink ash tray, 3-1/4", $15. *Courtesy of Kathy McCarney.*

Pink ash trays, bridge suits, queens, 3-1/2" x 2-3/4", set $35. *Courtesy of Valerie & Bill McCormack.*

Greensburg #2 pink "Elephant" ash tray, green and pink #1 "Terrier" ash trays, 6-1/4", $55 each. *Courtesy of Tracy Wills.*

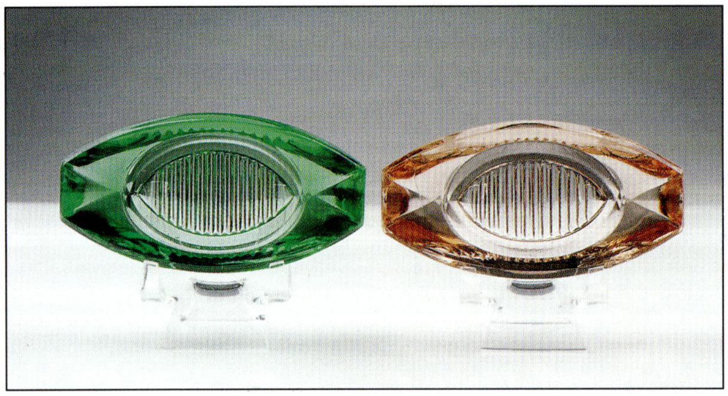

Pink and green ash trays, oval, 4-1/2", $10 each. *Courtesy of Tracy Wills.*

Amber and green ash trays, "Turtle" shaped, possibly Czechoslovakian, 4-1/4", $10 each. *Courtesy of Valerie & Bill McCormack.*

Amber ash tray, "Soccer Players" etched, 2-1/4" x 1-1/2", $20; amber "Angels" embossed ash tray, 2-1/4", $15. *Author's collection.*

Pink "Dice" ash tray, 1-3/4", $22. *Courtesy of Valerie & Bill McCormack.*

Fenton #1700 "Lincoln Inn" (1928-37) amber and aquamarine cigarette holders, 3", $35 each; amber and aquamarine ash trays, 2-1/2", $20 each. *Courtesy of Kathy McCarney.*

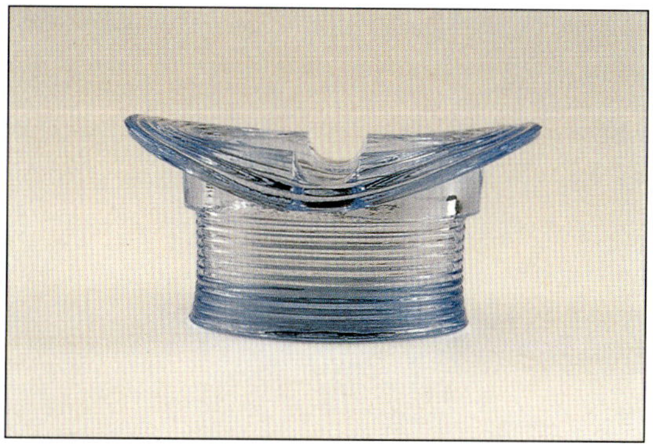

Cambridge #1903 "Top Hat" Willow blue ash tray, 1-1/2", $20. *Courtesy of Jeff & Mary Czech.*

Cobalt "Newcastle Exhibition" ash tray, produced in 1977 for the Golden Jubilee of Newcastle Brown Ale, 1927-77, 6", $25.

Hazel-Atlas cobalt ash tray, metal sailboat decoration, 5", $65. *Courtesy of Proctor's Depression Glass.*

Viking #412/1S "Swan" (c.1949) crystal with cobalt neck ash tray, handled, 4", $25. *Courtesy of Jeff & Mary Czech.*

Viking #996 "Horseshoe" Colonial blue ash tray, etched with Viking ship, 3", $15. *Author's collection.*

Fenton "Rose" Colonial green, Colonial amber, Colonial orange, Colonial blue #9271 ash trays, introduced by Fenton in 1966, 7-1/4", $10 each; ash tray sets, 4-1/4" ash tray; 4-1/4" x 3-3/4" tray, $25 each. *Courtesy of Donna Hatch.*

Fenton "Freeform/Swirl" Vaseline, Topaz, Wisteria, Spring green, Red Moonstone, Colonial blue, Colonial green ash trays, 4-3/4", $10 to $45 each; large ash trays Wisteria, red, $30 each. *Courtesy of Donna Hatch.*

Pink, green, smoke, blue ash trays, possibly Czechoslovakian, 3-1/4", set $20. *Courtesy of Valerie & Bill McCormack.*

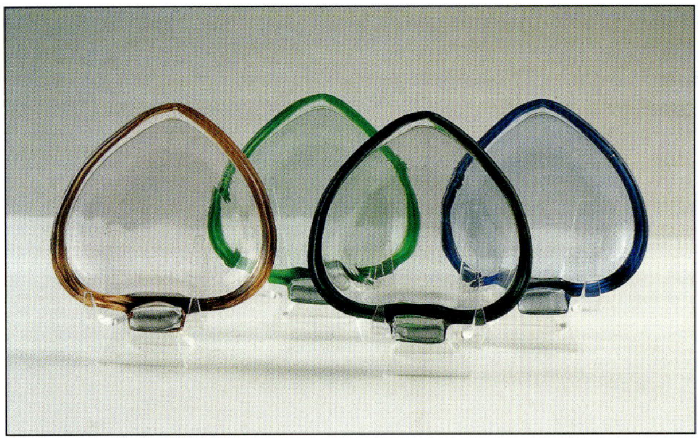

Hocking "Forest Green" ash trays, 3-1/2", 4-1/2", 6", set $25. *Author's collection.*

Jadite pipe rest ash tray, 5-1/2", $65. *Courtesy of Valerie & Bill McCormack.*

Green deco ash tray, slag glass, 5-1/4" x 3-1/2", $35. *Author's collection.*

Jeannette #530 (c.1938) jadite and delphite ash trays, with or without match book holders, 3-3/4", $35 each. *Courtesy of Valerie & Bill McCormack.*

Houze yellow/custard with brown and tan veining ash tray, white metal German Shepherd figural, 2-1/2" high, 3-1/2" wide, $55. *Courtesy of Valerie & Bill McCormack.*

Houze yellow/custard with brown and tan veining ash tray, 7-1/2" x 4-1/4", white metal lion figural, 3", $55. *Courtesy of Valerie & Bill McCormack.*

Houze yellow/custard with brown and tan veining ash tray, deco, octagonal with metal handle, 4" high, 5" wide, $30. *Courtesy of Valerie & Bill McCormack.*

Houze yellow/custard with brown and tan veining playing card trays, ace of each suit, original box, 3-3/4" x 2-1/4", $85. Each tray could be used as an ash tray or to identify the trump suit in bridge. *Courtesy of Valerie & Bill McCormack.*

Houze yellow/custard with brown and tan veining ash tray, metal flip top, 2-1/4", $30. *Courtesy of Valerie & Bill McCormack.*

Houze yellow/custard with brown and tan veining ash tray set, round, stacking, 3", set of four $22. Would originally have been housed in a brass holder. *Courtesy of Valerie & Bill McCormack.*

Houze Nile green (jadite) with brown marbleizing automobile dash ash tray, rubber suction cup, 3-1/4", $45; yellow/custard with orange marbleizing automobile dash ash tray, 3", $45. These are pictured upside down. *Courtesy of Valerie & Bill McCormack.*

Houze yellow/custard with brown and tan veining automobile ash tray, embossed "Mfg by Jos. Pollak Co. Pat. Pend. Boston Mass.," with metal clamp and lid, 4-3/4", $55. *Courtesy of Valerie & Bill McCormack.*

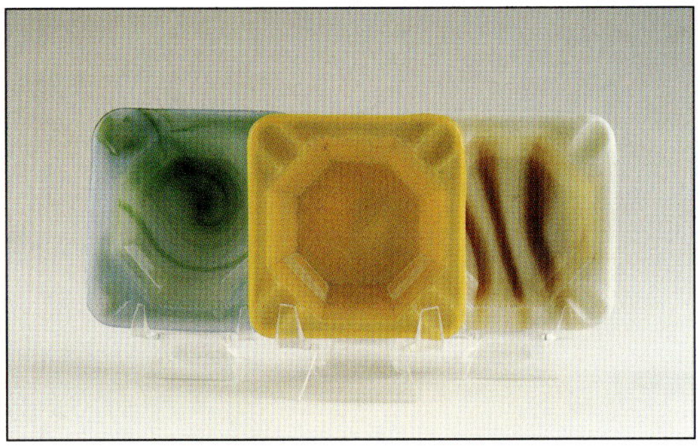

Akro Agate #252 ash tray, marbleized green and white; solid yellow; marbleized brown on custard, square, 3", $12 each. *Courtesy of Kathy McCarney.*

Akro Agate #249 ash trays, rectangular, marked, marbleized blue and white; green and white; blue, orange, and white, 2" x 4", $10 each. *Author's collection.*

Akro Agate #245 "Leaf" ash trays, "Made in USA 245," marbleized: Front row: green and white, green and white, brown and white; Back row: green and brown on custard, blue and white, $12 each. *Courtesy of Kathy McCarney.*

Akro Agate #252 marbleized ash trays, square, 3": Oxblood and white, $25; cobalt and white, $15; cigarette or match holders, 3", $15 each. *Courtesy of Kathy McCarney.*

Akro Agate embossed ash tray, 4", with match holder: blue "Hotel Edison" (New York), $85; green "Hotel Lincoln" (New York), $55.

Fenton "Rose" #9271 crystal ash tray, original label, 7-1/2", $12. *Courtesy of Donna Hatch.*

Crystal "Sailboat" ash tray, with metal sail, 6-1/4" high, 6" long, $30. *Courtesy of Tracy Wills.*

"Scottie Dogs" crystal ash tray, 5-1/2", $20. *Author's collection.*

"Fox Terrier" crystal ash tray, 3" x 2-1/4", $15. *Author's collection.*

Duncan Miller #30 "Pall Mall" (1930s-50s) crystal ash trays, duck shape: 7", $25; 4-3/4", $20; 4-1/2", $20; cigarette box, covered, 6", $45. Designed by Robert A. May.

Duncan Miller #32 crystal ash tray, "Mallard Duck Design" silver intaglio etching (1940s), oval, 5-1/2" x 3-1/2", $20. *Courtesy of David C. Cooper.*

Fostoria #2056 "American" (1915-86) crystal ash tray, oval, 3-3/4" x 2", $8. *Courtesy of Tracy Wills.*

Crystal ash tray, round, with match book holder, possibly Jeannette or Hocking, 4", $12. *Courtesy of Tracy Wills.*

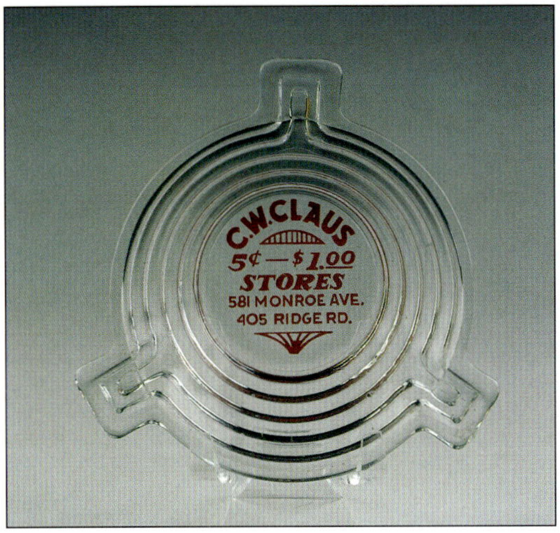

Hocking "Manhattan" (1938-43) crystal ash tray, round, "C. W. Claus 5¢ - $1.00 Stores 581 Monroe Ave. 405 Ridge Rd. (Rochester)," 4", $15. *Courtesy of Kathy McCarney.*

Hocking "Waterford" (1938-44) crystal ash tray, round, "Post Cereals," 4", $12. *Courtesy of Kathy McCarney.*

Libbey "Safedge" crystal ash trays, round, "Rhum Negrita," "New England Hotel Exposition Boston April 1937," 4", $12 each. Libbey introduced their "Safedge Glassware" in 1924, guaranteeing "a new glass if the rim ever chips." *Author's collection.*

Viking #436 "Swan" Ebony (black) ash tray, with crystal handle, 5-1/2", $25. *Courtesy of Jeff & Mary Czech.*

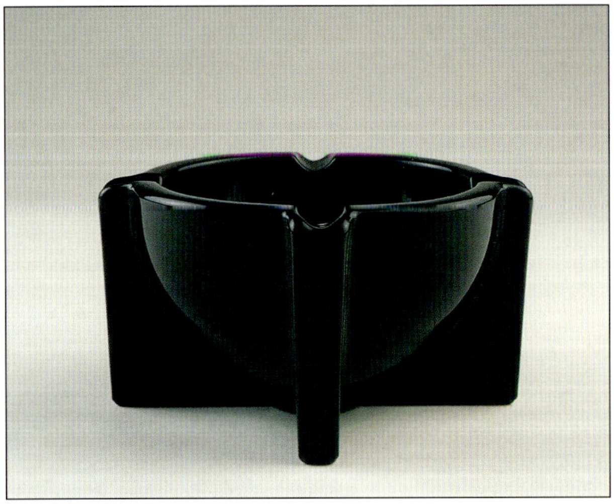

Fry black ash tray, deco, 5", $35. *Courtesy of Valerie & Bill McCormack.*

Cambridge #390 (c.1940) Ebony (black) ash tray, silver overlay monogram "GD", 6", $35. *Courtesy of Dale Basaraba.*

Cambridge "Chantilly" (1936-58) ash tray, sterling silver base, 3-1/4", $25. Made from the coaster mold but crimped as a special order for a silver company. A cigarette holder was also made from the "Chantilly" pattern. *Courtesy of Suzanne Fry.*

Greensburg #2 "Elephant" black ash tray, 6-1/4", $55. *Courtesy of Francois Houle.*

Black "Scottie Dog" ash tray, 4-3/4" x 4-3/4", $55. *Author's collection.*

Duncan Miller "Duck" milk glass ash tray, 8" long, $125.

Fenton #9271 "Talsman Rose" milk glass #9210 ash tray set in holder, 4-1/4", $55; lighter, 4", $35; large ash tray, 7-1/4", $35. Made for Sears. *Courtesy of Donna Hatch.*

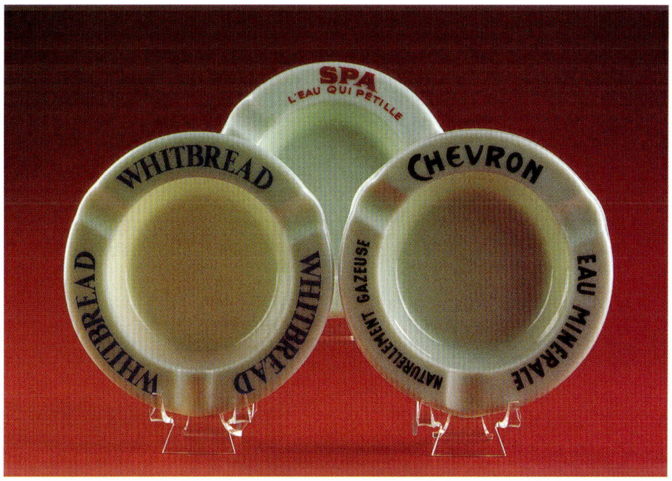

European jadite ash trays, "Whitbread," "Spa," "Chevron," 6", $25 each. *Author's collection.*

Fenton "Freeform" Moonstone ash tray, 6", $55. *Courtesy of Donna Hatch.*

Tire Ash Trays

Tire ash trays are one of those collectibles that cut across more than one collector category. Automobile enthusiasts, from vintage to modern, as well as glass collectors whose favorite companies provided the inserts for these novel items all are in the hunt.

The very first ash tray tire was made in 1915 for the Pennsylvania Rubber Company, Jeannette, Pennsylvania—their Vacuum Cup Tire Ash Tray. The glass insert was produced for them by the Hocking Glass Company of Lancaster, Ohio. Akro Agate was another of the favorite glass companies that made such inserts. These tire ash trays were made as customer giveaways, as sales incentives, for top dealerships, as as tokens of service to retirees. Firestone made commemorative tire ash trays for the 1934 Chicago World's Fair and the 1936 Texas Centennial, amongst other celebrations. The rarest of tire ash trays can run well over a hundred dollars in price, while newer or more common examples can be found for several dollars. These items fall into that group of collectibles that one simply does not expect to be so popular; it is amazing how many people are fascinated by them.

"Firestone" amber ash tray, rubber tire rim, 4-1/4", $35. "Goodrich" amber ash tray, 4-1/4", $45. *Courtesy of Pat Kurtz.*

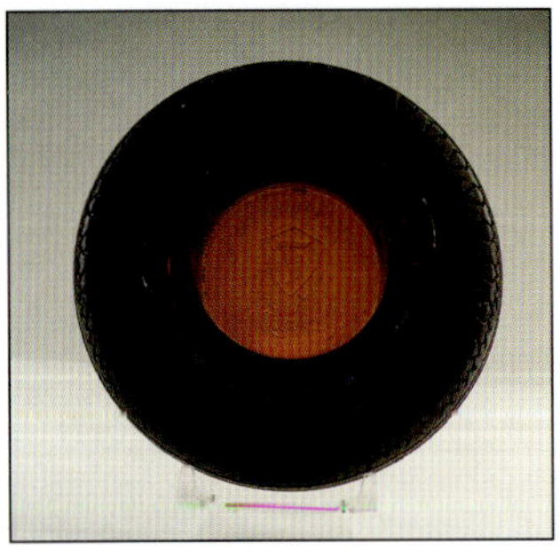

"Firestone" amber tire ash tray, 6", $35. *Courtesy of Valerie & Bill McCormack.*

"B.F. Goodrich" crystal tire ash tray, tan and black logo, 6", $20; crystal "Dunlop" tire ash tray, tan and black logo, 6", $20. *Courtesy of Pat Kurtz.*

"Cooper" 75 years of quality (1914-89), black and white logo, 6", $20. *Courtesy of Pat Kurtz.*

"Remington" crystal tire ash tray, green and black logo, 6", $15; "Transit tire" crystal tire ash tray, yellow and black logo, 6", $15. *Courtesy of Pat Kurtz.*

"General Tire" crystal tire ash tray, 6" yellow and black logo, $15; "General Tire" crystal tire ash tray, black and white logo, 6", $20. *Courtesy of Pat Kurtz.*

"Good Year" crystal tire ash tray, white and blue logo, 6", $15; yellow and blue logo, 6", $20. *Courtesy of Pat Kurtz.*

"Seasonmaster" crystal tire ash tray, 6", $15; "Firestone" crystal tire ash tray, 6", $20. *Courtesy of Pat Kurtz.*

Appendix A

Canadian Depression Glass Association

The Canadian Depression Glass Association (CDGA) provides information about Depression Glass and related topics to fellow "Preservationists of Depression Era Glassware." As well, the CDGA provides a marketplace for the sale of and the search for Depression Glass. The voice of the CDGA is the *Canadian Depression Glass Review*, published six times a year. Established in 1976, the CDGA has members from coast to coast in Canada, and in the United States. Originally the CDGA was formed in Western Canada as the Prairie Depression Glass Club (by mail). We encourage all members to contribute to the advancement of Depression Glass knowledge.

Memberships: $20 per year or $50 for three years.

Checks or money orders payable to the Canadian Depression Glass Association should be sent to:

CDGA
P.O. Box 41564
HLRPO, 230 Sandalwood Pkwy
Brampton, Ontario
L6Z 4R1 CANADA
(905) 846-2835
www.waltztime.com/CDGA

Toronto Depression Glass Show & Sales

Twice yearly on the first Sunday in May and November, from 10 am to 4 pm

Barware, Adam to Windsor, Corn Flower, Elegant Glass, Fire-King, Kitchen Glass
Glass Displays and Free Identification Clinics

Location:
German Canadian Club Hansa
6650 Hurontario Street
Mississauga, Ontario
L5W 1N3 CANADA

Sponsored by Waltz Time Antiques
For further information, contact:
(905) 846-2835
walt@waltztime.com
www.waltztime.com

Appendix B

Glossary of Barware Terms

The measurements for capacity or height of barware items are simply averages. You are bound to find exceptions to the rule.

Barbell. A dumbbell or barbell-shaped cocktail shaker, made by West Virginia Glass Specialty

Bitters Bottle. Around 8 oz., bottles topped with a metal tube device held in with a cork collar, for dispensing small portions of liquors.

Brandy Inhaler/Snifter. From 2 oz. to a massive 100+ oz., traditional stemmed, rounded bowl shape.

Coaster. 3-1/4" to 4-1/2" usually round, ribbed plate for placing drinks on to protect furniture.

Champagne.

Saucer Champagne. 5-1/2 oz., original French style, now more for champagne cocktails.

Hollow Stem Champagne. 5 oz., goblet shape, makes for a real show of bubbles traveling up the long throat of the hollow stem.

Champagne Flute or Goblet. 5-1/2 oz., style most in favor currently, often long stemmed and narrow with bowl curving inwards.

Cocktail. 4 to 6 oz., goblet with flared bowl.

Cocktail Shaker. Approximately 32 oz., usually cylindrical container for shaking up contents for cocktails, sometimes handled; boot-shaped shakers are highly sought after.

Cordial/Liqueur. 1 oz., small stemmed glass, often with rounded sides.

Crème de Menthe. 2 oz., narrow bowl that widens out, a "Ladies Cocktail."

Decanter. 16 to 36 oz., an ornamental glass bottle for serving wine or liquors.

Hi Ball Tumbler/Tom Collins/Shell Glass (alternatively hiball, high ball, etc.). 8 to 12 oz. straight, tall glasses, usually thin-sided.

Ice Bucket. Approximately 6" in height, handled cylindrical container for ice cubes.

Ice Tub. Approximately 3-1/2" in height, cylindrical, often tab handled.

Muddler. Rod for mashing mint, fruits, or sugars in a cocktail.

Old-Fashioned. 8 to 10 oz., flat bottomed tumbler, often with sham base, generally straight flared sides.

Pilsener Beer. 9-1/2 oz., stemmed, thin, tapering glass.

Pousse Café. 1-1/2 to 2-1/2 oz., tall, slender footed glass, a drink with distinct layers of ingredients.

Punch Set. Large bowl for punch or egg nog, sometimes with stand, a ladle, and 8 or 12 handled mugs, often in opaque glass (milk glass, jadite, custard).

Reamer. Ribbed conical device used for the squeezing

of citrus fruit for juices.

Recipe Shaker. A cocktail shaker with cocktail recipes as the decoration.

Samovar. Large containers for dispensing beverages (coffee, whiskey, wine). Depression era samovars are usually glass containers in metal frames.

Sham Base. Thick glass base in tumblers, cocktail shakers, etc.

Sherry. 2 to 3 oz., generally a goblet with flared edges.

Skyscraper. A super tall cocktail shaker, usually 14"+

Swizzle. A stick used for stirring mixed drinks.

Tire Ash Tray. Rubber advertising ash tray with glass insert, made since 1915.

Tom Collins. 14 oz., a tall drink with lots of room for ice and all.

Tom & Jerry. 4-1/2 oz. handled mug, often made with opaque glass (custard, milk glass, etc.).

Whiskey Tumbler/Shot Glass/Jigger. Around 1-1/2 oz., used more as a measuring tumbler than for drinking, often with sham base.

Appendix C
Glass Companies

Akro Agate (1914-1951), Clarksburg, West Virginia

Bartlett-Collins (1914-present), Sapulpa, Oklahoma

Bryce Brothers Company (1896-1967), Mt. Pleasant, Pennsylvania

A.H. Cambridge Glass Company (1901-1958), Cambridge, Ohio

Central Glass Works (1896-1939), Wheeling, West Virginia

Consolidated Lamp & Glass Company (1894-1967), Coraopolis, Pennsylvania

Dell Glass Company (1940s), Millville, New Jersey

Diamond Glass-Ware Company (1891-1931), Indiana, Pennsylvania

Dunbar Flint Glass Corporation (1913-1953), Dunbar, West Virginia

George Duncan & Sons (1874-1891), Washington, Pennsylvania

Duncan Miller Glass Company (1893-1955), Washington, Pennsylvania

Federal Glass Company (1900-1984), Columbus, Ohio

Fenton Art Glass (1905-present), Williamstown, West Virginia

Fostoria Glass Company (1887-1986), Moundsville, Ohio

H. C. Fry Glass Company (1901-1933), Rochester, Pennsylvania

Greensburg Glass/L.E. Smith (1907-2004), Mt. Pleasant, Pennsylvania

Hazel-Atlas Glass (1902-1984), Washington, Pennsylvania

A.H. Heisey and Company (1893-1958), Newark, Ohio

Hocking Glass Company (1905-present), Lancaster, Ohio

L. J. Houze Convex Glass Company (1914-2005), Point Marion, Pennsylvania

W. J. Hughes (1914-1988), Toronto, Canada

Imperial Glass Corporation (1904-1984), Bellaire, Ohio

Indiana Glass Company (1907-2002), Dunkirk, Indiana

Jeannette Glass Company (1898-1983), Jeannette, Pennsylvania

Libbey Glass Company (1892-present), Toledo, Ohio

Liberty Works (1903-1932), Egg Harbor, New Jersey

MacBeth-Evans (1899-1937), Charleroi, Pennsylvania

McKee Glass Company (1888-1967), Jeannette, Pennsylvania

Morgantown Glass Works (1903-1975), Morgantown, West Virginia

New Martinsville Glass Company (1901-1944), New Martinsville, West Virginia

Paden City Glass Manufacturing Company (1916-1951), Paden City, West Virginia

Seneca Glass Company (1891-1983), Morgantown West Virginia

Tiara Company/Indiana Glass (1970-1998), Dunkirk, Indiana

Tiffin Glass Company (1888-1962), Tiffin, Ohio

U.S. Glass Company (1891-1962), Pittsburgh, Pennsylvania

Vidrio Products Corporation (c.1929-1953), Chicago, Illinois

Viking Glass Company (1944-1986), New Martinsville, West Virginia

Thos. Webb & Sons (1840-1986), Stourbridge, UK

West Virginia Glass Specialty (1930-1987), Weston, West Virginia

Westmoreland Glass Company (1889-1984), Westmoreland, Pennsylvania

Appendix D

The Edward Harris House Inn

Enjoy the quiet elegance of this urban inn located in the heart of the historic arts and cultural district of Rochester, New York. Walk wonderful tree lined streets to area boutiques, restaurants, galleries and museums.

The Edward Harris House was built as a wedding present form Mr. Harris to his daughter, Emily Harris Sloan, in 1896. Mr. Harris was the co-founder of the Harris, Beach law firm, which is the oldest still existing law firm in Rochester.

The home's exquisite workmanship and detail are hallmarks of the celebrated architect, Claude Bragdon, who designed the home early in his career. Both Mr. Harris and Mr. Bragdon worked with George Eastman, founder of the Eastman-Kodak Corp.

The Edward Harris House Inn
35 Argyle Street
Rochester, New York 14607

Phone: (585) 473-9752
Toll Free: (800) 419-1213
EHHBB@aol.com
www.edwardharrishousebb.com

Selected Bibliography

Bergreen, Laurence. *Capone: The Man and the Era*. New York: Simon & Schuster, 1994.

Bickenheuser, Fred. *Tiffin Glass Masters*. Grove City, Ohio: Glass Masters Publications, 1979.

Bickenheuser, Fred. *Tiffin Glass Masters Volume II*. Grove City, Ohio: Glass Masters Publications, 1981.

Bones, Frances. *Duncan Glass*. Des Moines, Iowa: Wallace Homestead Book Company, 1973.

Bredehoft, Neila & Tom. *Heisey Glass 1896-1957*. Paducah, Kentucky: Collector Books, 2001.

Bredehoft, Neila. *Heisey Glass 1925-1938*. Paducah, Kentucky: Collector Books, 1986.

Coe, Debbie & Randy. *Elegant Glass: Early, Depression, and Beyond*, 2nd edition. Atglen, Pennsylvania: Schiffer Publishing Ltd., 2004.

Florence, Gene. *Collector's Encyclopedia of Depression Glass*, 16th edition. Paducah, Kentucky: Collector Books, 2004.

Florence, Gene. *Elegant Glassware of the Depression Era*, 10th edition. Paducah, Kentucky: Collector Books, 2003.

Gallagher, Jerry. *Handbook of Old Morgantown Glass*. Minneapolis, Minnesota: Merit Printing, 1995.

Garrison, Myrna and Bob. *Candlewick: The Crystal Line*. Atglen, Pennsylvania: Schiffer Publishing Ltd., 2003.

Gervais, C.H. *The Rumrunners: A Prohibition Scrapbook*. Scarborough, Ontario: Firefly Books, 1984.

Goshe, Ed, Ruth Hemminger, & Leslie Piña. *Tiffin Depression Era Stems & Tableware*. Atglen, Pennsylvania: Schiffer Publishing Ltd., 1998.

Hunt, Claude William. *Booze, Boats and Billions: Smuggling Liquid Gold*. Toronto, Ontario: McClelland and Stewart, 1988.

Kobler, John. *Capone: the life and world of Al Capone*. New York: Collier Books, 1971.

Long, Milbra and Emily Seate. *Fostoria Tableware, 1924-1943*. Paducah, Kentucky: Collector Books, 1999.

Long, Milbra and Emily Seate. *Fostoria Useful & Ornamental*. Paducah, Kentucky: Collector Books, 2000.

Kovar, Lorraine. *Westmoreland Glass, Volume 3, 1888-1940*. Marietta, Ohio: Glass Press, 1997.

Krause, Gail. *Duncan Glass*. Smithtown, New York: Exposition Press, 1976.

Mauzy, Barbara and Jim. *Mauzy's Depression Glass*, 3rd edition. Atglen, Pennsylvania: Schiffer Publishing Ltd., 2004.

Measell, James. *New Martinsville Glass, 1900-1944*. Marietta, Ohio: Antique Publications, 1994.

Measell, James, ed. *Imperial Glass Encyclopedia, Vol. I.* National Imperial Glass Collector's Society. Marietta, Ohio: The Glass Press Inc., 1995.

Measell, James, ed. *Imperial Glass Encyclopedia, Vol. II.* National Imperial Glass Collector's Society. Marietta, Ohio: The Glass Press Inc., 1997.

Measell, James, ed. *Imperial Glass Encyclopedia, Vol. III.* National Imperial Glass Collector's Society. Marietta, Ohio: The Glass Press Inc., 1999.

Measell, James and Berry Wiggins. *Great American Glass of the Roaring 20s & Depression Era.* Marietta, Ohio: Antique Publications, 1998.

National Cambridge Collectors. *Colors in Cambridge Glass.* Paducah, Kentucky: Collector Books, 1984.

National Cambridge Collectors. *Reprint of 1930-34 Catalog.* Paducah, Kentucky: Collector Books, 1976.

National Cambridge Collectors. *Reprint of 1949 thru 1953 Catalog.* Paducah, Kentucky: Collector Books, 1978.

Nye, Mark, ed. *Reprint of 1940 Cambridge Glass Company Catalog.* Cambridge, Ohio: National Cambridge Collectors, 1995.

Piña, Leslie. *Depression Era Glass by Duncan.* Atglen, Pennsylvania: Schiffer Publishing Ltd., 1999.

Piña, Leslie, and Jerry Gallagher. *Tiffin Glass 1914-1940.* Atglen, Pennsylvania: Schiffer Publishing Ltd., 1996.

Six, Dean. *Viking Glass 1944-1970.* Atglen, Pennsylvania: Schiffer Publishing Ltd., 2003.

Six, Dean. *West Virginia Glass Between the World Wars.* Atglen, Pennsylvania: Schiffer Publishing Ltd., 2002.

Snyder, Jeffrey B. *Morgantown Glass: From Depression Glass Through the 1960s.* Atglen, Pennsylvania: Schiffer Publishing Ltd. 1998.

Torsiello, Paul & Debora, and Tom & Arlene Stillman. *Paden City Glassware.* Atglen, Pennsylvania: Schiffer Publishing Ltd., 2002.

Visakay, Stephen. *Vintage Bar Ware.* Paducah, Kentucky: Collector Books, 1997.

Walker, William P., Melissa Bratkovich, and Joan C. Walker. *Paden City Glass Company 1916-1951.* Marietta, Ohio: Antique Publications, 2003.

Warsh, Cheryl Krasnick, ed. *Drink in Canada: Historical Essays.* Montreal, Quebec: McGill-Queen's University Press, 1993.

Weatherman, Hazel Marie. *Colored Glassware of the Depression Era 2*, Springfield, Missouri: Weatherman Glassbooks, 1974.

Weatherman, Hazel Marie. *Fostoria the First 50 Years.* Springfield, Missouri: Weatherman Glass Books, 1974.

Whitmyer, Kenn & Margaret. *Fenton Art Glass Patterns 1939-80.* Paducah, Kentucky: Collector Books, 1999.

Wilson, Jack. *Phoenix & Consolidated Glass.* Marietta, Ohio: Antique Publications, 1989.

Yeakley, Virginia & Loren. *Heisey Glass in Color.* Marietta, Ohio: Richardson Printing Corporation, 1978.

Index